AMEDEO STORTI

ROME

A PRACTICAL GUIDE

WITH MAPS - 48 COLOUR PLATES

EXCURSION ITINERARIES

To see Rome in one or two days, select the monuments you prefer from the sketch below and, beyond the third day, follow the itineraries described in the guide. Means of transportation: page 124. First day (line 1-12): 1. **ST. PETER'S** (page 25). Interior, Dome. Michelangelo's Pietà. 2 **SQUARE**. 3. **SISTINE CHAPEL** (page 38): frescoes by Michelangelo. 4. **BELVEDERE** (page 36). Statues: Laocöon, Apollo, Torso. 5. **The RAPHAEL ROOMS** (page 42). 6. **JANICULUM** (page 51) Pause for lunch (page 126). 7. **FORO ITALICO** (page 48). 8. **PIAZZA NAVONA** (page 87): Fountain of the Rivers (Bernini). 9. **PANTHEON** (page 85): the representative building of Ancient Rome. 10 **ARA PACIS** (page 92). 11. **PIAZZA DEL POPOLO** (page 92). 12. **PIAZZA DI SPAGNA** (page 94) Second day (Segmented line 13-22): 13. **CAPITOLINE HILL** (page 55). Statue of Marcu Aurelius. New Wing. Statues: Venus, Dying Gaul; Mosaic of the Doves. Palazzo dei Conservatori

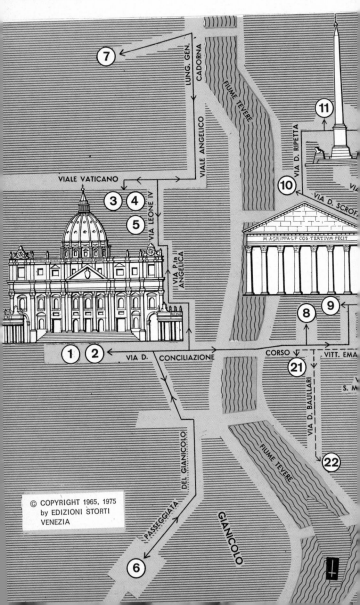

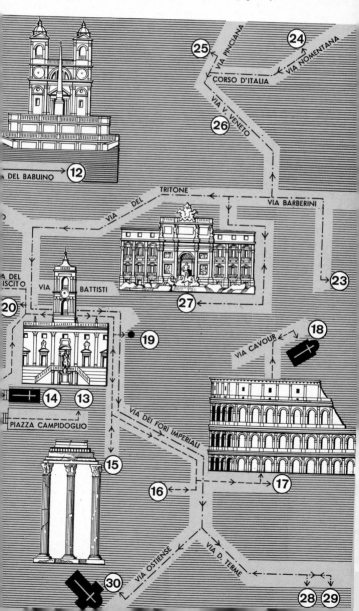

Farnesina

Forum of Caesar Via del Corso

Roman Forum

Column of Trajan

Libraries

Basilica Ulpia

Church of Ss. Nome di M

n's Market   Villa Madama   Tower of the Milizie   Quirinale Palace

ori Imperiali   Temple of Mars Ultor   Forum of Augustus   Forum Transitorium

ANECDOTES AND CURIOSITIES

The Oracle. On leaving for the wars, a soldier together with his wife and children wished to hear the judgement of the oracle. After entrusting his offering to the guardian, he humbly pronounced the ritual formula; and in the silence broken only by the children's chatter the response was heard:

« Go, you shall return — NOT — in battle shall you die! »

Roman Spirit. Caesar was sorely distressed at his lack of hair, and one of his vices was lechery. During the triumph accorded him following the conquest of Gaul, the legionaries mocked the general's defects before a cheering crowd as was the custom. Caesar let slip a gesture of irritation and resentment; and the soldiers, now even more delighted, jeered openly, « Citizens: look out for your wives, he whom we accompany is adulterous and bald! »

Superstition. The Roman like all peoples of antiquity was superstitious, most probably because his particular mode of intercourse with the divinity consented to this attitude. His world and even his daily life were filled with spirits that invaded man and his home with evil spells, some of which survive to this day, with rituals and exorcism to obtain favours or avert demons. The rituals were linked with the afterlife whose tangible intermediaries were the blood and bones of the dead. The « Mouth of Truth » is one of the many examples of popular superstition.

Water, aqueducts, fountains. Rome is a city of water, and it animates her in a number of ways, splashing exuberantly down her slopes in cascades, garrulously filling sarcophagi in squares, courtyards and streets, rising in spouts and tumbling in foam over statues and fountains. A wealth of literature and symphonic poetry testifies to this special aspect of the city's beauty.

Roads, bridges, cloacae. During the Empire, Rome's streets were paved with basalt rock fixed in cement. A vast network of roads, bearing the names of consuls who had them constructed — consular roads: Flaminia, Cassia, Aemilia, Aurelia, Appia — joined her to the provinces of the vast empire. Another admirable accomplishment of Roman building techniques was the bridge. Nine of them link the banks of the Tiber: Elio or S. Angelo, Neroniano, Agrippa, Aurelio or Ponte Sisto, Fabricio or dei 4 Capi, Cestio, Aemilio or Ponte Rotto, Sublicio, Probo. A complex system of sewers emptied the city's refuse into the Tiber, rendering Imperial Rome very similar to any modern city. The Cloaca Maxima, whose outlet may be seen near the Palatine Bridge, is considered the first of its kind (6th cent. B. C.).

Church of S. Pietro in Vincoli.
Michelangelo Buonarroti: Moses

1

2

3

4

5

6

NOTES ON THE STYLES

Arch and Vault

The semi-circular **Arch** and the **Vault,** architectural elements that join two points in space, reach their maximum development in the aqueducts, bridges and in nearly all constructions of the Roman era. Known from antiquity and employed with rare skill by those great masters of the Romans, the Etruscans, they endow Roman architecture with that character of forceful solidity and order which reflect the organizing genius of their builders. They are the essential motif of Roman architecture and constitute its glory.

The styles found in Roman art in its various periods are direct derivations of the classic style: columns and semi-circular arches. The **Orders,** of Greek origin, are classified thus: **Doric, Ionic** and **Corinthian,** from the name of the people who created them or the city where they flourished; and they are distinguished by the varying proportions of the column shaft and the different decorations of the capital.

The **Styles,** which show their classical derivation in the very names which define them, are distinguished by the diverse proportions of the arch, its relation to the dimensions of the columns, and by the decoration.

They are called.

Byzantine, from the 6th—9th cent.;

Romanesque, from the 10th—15th cent.;

Renaissance, 15th—16th cent.;

Baroque, 17th—18th cent.;

Neo-Classic, 19th cent.;

Neo-Empire, 20th cent.

Rome's only complete construction in **Gothic** style — pointed arch —, born in France in the 12th cent. and developed in Europe, is the church of S. Maria Sopra Minerva. Also in this style are a few ciboriums and windows in other parts of the city.

Doric	1
Ionic	2
Corinthian	3
4 Semi-circular Arch	
5 Pointed Arch	
Tunnel Vault	6

Vatican Gardens

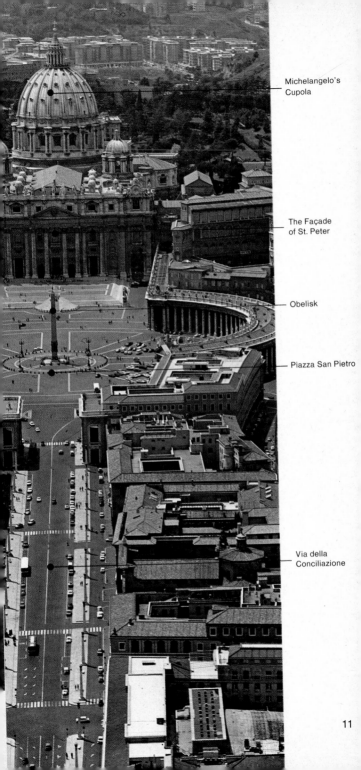

Michelangelo's
Cupola

The Façade
of St. Peter

Obelisk

Piazza San Pietro

Via della
Conciliazione

11

INTRODUCTION

The institutions which lend to the 2700 year old history of Rome an all together universal character are the **Empire** and the **Papacy,** the one personified by the governing emperor, the other represented by the pope, who for a specified period invested others with the exercise of power. The Empire rose from a need to administer far-flung territories and to put an end to the struggle between rival factions; the papacy, in the chaos which dominated Europe with the fall of the Empire, was the only authority in the West to whom the desperate population looked with trust and from whom protection was expected. If the former owed its strength and, in time, its feebleness and fall to the unlimited powers assumed by the emperor, who while living was adored as a god, and at death was deified, the latter derived its particular authority directly from God as His representative on earth. The period of the Empire, then, represents the point of maximum development and the consequent decay of all the elements which compose the Roman as a spiritual and physical entity.

From the first the Roman was a typical warrior — Romulus slayed his brother Remus because he transgressed the law — and such he remained; and he was engaged in stock-raising. The origins of the city are lost in myth and legend. We do know, though, that during the period of the Kings, the Romans were for a time subjected to the Etruscans; and that the city underwent invasions (Gauls).

During the Republic (Res publica, Commonwealth) the government, entrusted to senators and people (S.P.Q.R.), was very strong and the army powerful. The city extended its dominion over the peoples of the Italic peninsula: Latins, Etruscans, Samnites, Lucanians, Greeks, and beyond, over Sicily, Carthage, Sardinia, Spain and Greece (340-133 B.C.). Rome was then overcrowded with wooden huts, to a greater degree on the Palatine (from the root, Pâ, as in Pales, goddess of shepherds), in the Subura, and along the river; the lanes were filled with refuse and animals. Life was led in the house amid the slaves, and in Campus Martius, among the legionaries.

The character of the times is personified by the consul, Manlius. In the battle of Vesuvius (340 B.C.) he had his son decapitated for having disobeyed an order — he had accepted a challenge from the enemy leader and defeated him.

The sober severe life of Cato is also indicative of the times. On the other hand, the Scipio family in their fondness for the Greek way of life, represent progress.

Among the customs of the epoch was that of inhumation: the dead were transported at night-time by torch light — the custom survives to this day — and cast into the immense Esquiline ditch.

Although these were the essential features of the Roman and of Rome, the conquests, the contact with peoples of refined culture — the Greeks —, and the changing economic situation led to progress and modified the character of the people and the face of the city.

Colosseum. Roman Road, Pavement

In Constantine's day (306-337) Rome was a city of one million inhabitants. It had two circuits of walls, 190 granaries, 250 gristmills, two general markets, eleven aqueducts, eleven forums, eleven baths, ten basilicas, thirty-six arches, 1150 fountains, twenty-eight libraries, two circuses, two amphitheatres. It was organized in districts, embellished with luxurious gardens, criss-crossed by paved streets where at corners and intersections were niches with statues of the gods; the custom still prevails.

City life was regulated by a few basic rules; the traffic of heavy carts was permitted only at night, a corps of policemen patrolled the streets, forums were usually frequented from eleven to one and the baths in the afternoon; the duties of daily life were performed in the morning. At night the city was perilous: carts often crushed passers-by against the walls; the refuse thrown from windows was another danger; bands of robbers kidnapped and sold people into slavery. By day, however, it was everywhere animated with intense life: from the constant and sometimes menacing hubbub of the Subura, the notorious popular quarter, to the brisk activity of the forums, and the chaotic traffic of the port: with merchandise displayed in the streets, and the noises and odours of the various trades — tanners, butchers, sword makers, barbers —; to the exercises of the city's youth in the Campus Martius and gymnasiums.

Slaves of all races and great quantities of merchandise, the contrasts of unlimited luxury and abject misery — a society based on slavery degrades human dignity — and forever crowded streets show a capital of refined but still primitive

14

civilization.

The Roman then assisted in ecstasy at the bloody spectacles of the circus, he was given to idleness and indulged in pleasure, complaining all the while of the dangers of army life. Corruption crept into Roman society; official accusations for obtaining inheritances of the dead were on the rise; and following the wild ventures of Caligula, Nero, Caracalla — to name only a few — the authority of the emperor was undermined and power passed first into the hands of the Praetorians and later was assumed by the army.

The Roman of the Empire is personified by Commodus, who in a street encountered a tall, robust gladiator and approaching him, ran him through with his sword. Such were the customs of the times that the crowd at the circus roared as the emperor turned thumbs down on the fallen victim; and at the exit no one bothered to glance at the long row of carts piled high with men and beasts killed for fun. The **Roman house** — one floor, two courtyards, round which the windowless construction was built, with shops on the exterior — was the last institution to yield its ancient atmosphere of serenity.

From the last century of the Republic to the Fall, this city saw such famous men as Caesar, Brutus, Cleopatra, Antony, Augustus, Maecenas, and Cicero, the orator, renowned poets like Virgil, Catullus, Horace, wise emperors of Trajan's stamp, perverts like Nero and Caligula and brave men on a par with Septimius Severus, Aurelian, Diocletian.

But besides the moral dissatisfaction which people attempted to dull, drowning their lives in pleasure, in the city appeared

Buildings in Rome (Plastic model of the town of Rome at the time of Constantine)

the first sprouts of Christianity, a religion which warms the spirit, while the Barbarians, who for some time had constituted the core of the army pressed at the borders.

This historical cycle concluded in bloodshed, ruin and anarchy.

Rome mirrored conditions throughout the peninsula and Europe.

Following the penetration of the first barbarians, those elements which were to constitute the city's new historical context engaged in a struggle for power: the noble Roman was practically swept away — though at least in Rome, the Latins predominated —, the barbarian — Huns, Goths, Angles, Franks, Lombards, Saxons —, the luxurious Byzantine, and the Christian organization of the Papacy.

The conflict lasted over nine centuries, from the official fall of Rome (Odoacer, 475) to the return of the Popes from Avignon (1377), and plunged the city into the desperate conditions of the 8th, 9th, 10th cent., during which time even the chronicles grew silent and the survivors lived like beasts.

Gregory the Great, survivor of a noble Roman family (Anici), led barefoot through the mud the long procession of submission for the cessation of the plague, and the Angel sheathed its flaming sword above the Mausoleum of Hadrian, thenceforth known as Castel S. Angelo. These Romans, of ancient senatorial tradition, brought the Papacy to effective force on Christmas Day in the year 800.

With the constitution of the Holy Roman Empire, the Euro-

pean nations accepted the ancient principle of the Roman Empire, the mediating function of the pope and the people of Rome (S.P.Q.R.): and so Western barbarism came into contact with Roman culture and civilization.

In the 10th century a grotesque event took place: the ragamuffins ranged themselves along the pathways of Rome, then a village, and applauded the passage of a man crowned with laurel. Gloating like a satyr he pranced before the corpse of his twentieth wife.

Excesses of all sorts prevailed, from the pilgrimage trend to the search for relics, from the struggle of families for the conquest of the Papacy to the interferences of various emperors and the destruction of monuments. But amid the anarchy and upheavals of those long centuries, the church collected and preserved, sanctified and handed down.

Rome with its 60.000 inhabitants had undergone a profound transformation and offered a heart-rending spectacle. The vast area within the walls was overgrown with orchards and fields; pigs and sheep roamed the footpaths obstructed with marbles and statues; the Forum was deserted and vegetation crept along the columns; on the arches and in the theatres fortresses were built. Streets were blocked and districts inaccessible; armed bands guarded the gates.

No one felt safe: riches, possessions, persons had little or no value. Sheep grazed at the threshold of St. Peter's.

Toward the end of this period three noble popes came to the fore, Gregory VII, Innocent III and Boniface VIII; a popular hero, Cola di Rienzo, who died like a buffoon, a Saint, Catherine of Siena; a painter, Giotto; a poet, Dante.

The stadium of Nero, or, in later times, Piazza San Pietro (Plastic model of the town of Rome at the time of Constantine).

The golden era of the Papacy began with the return from Avignon and ended with the Sack (1527). In that century the Papacy, then free from the interference of the people and with the struggles of noble families quenched, arrived by alliances at deciding the destiny of numerous Italian principalities and European nations.

A great number of famous men succeeded one another to the throne of St. Peter: the Borgia, Callixtus IV and Alexander VI; the Della Rovere, Sixtus IV and Julius II; the Piccolomini, Pius II and Pius III; the Medici, Leo X and Clement VII; and with them the city was flooded with Spaniards, Genoese, Sienese, Florentines who inhabited the center. The Romans played no part, perhaps because the Orsini-Colonna families were conscious of the fact that if the one gained favour the other would perish.

A momentous event shook all Europe at the start of the new century: the demolition of the old and the construction of the new St. Peter's. The works carried out in this period, though, did not transform the city. In fact, ruins were being recovered, the long convent walls impeded an organic system of construction, and the Tiber periodically flooded the foundations of buildings.

The **Palace** was a typical construction of the epoch. It comprised, among other elements, a façade and a courtyard, embellished with columns and decorated with marbles, statues and sarcophagi removed from ancient monuments and adapted for use as fountains. The numerous, spacious rooms were animated with a particular atmosphere by colour and fresco motifs — scenes from antiquity and episodes of current history in the manner of the ancients —, by stuccoes of refined technique, by the furniture whose solid, robust structure bespoke the secular tradition of the craft guilds.

People gathered in the streets where social life took place and these arteries traversed the districts of Ponte, Parione Pigna, S. Eustachio, Campo Marzio, Campitelli. Obvious contrasts split the classes: nobles, clergy, people. This was particularly apparent during the festivals in the church of SS. Apostoli; and corruption spread. The greater part of the population continued to live overshadowed by the immense riches that flowed into Rome from all parts of Europe. The life of the times may be summed up in the festivals organized for the arrival of a prince, for the marriage of a princess and in the excesses perpetrated during the sack of the city. At that time Rome was a centre of attraction for poets, architects, sculptors, literati who came here especially from Florence and from Europe at large. Filarete, Pinturicchio, Pollaiuolo, but above all the giants whose creations led the Humanistic - Renaissance movement to its technical - artistic climax: Michelangelo, Raphael, Bramante. The lives of these artists, the enmities that divided them, the contrasts between their artistic convictions, and the complex demands of popes, princes, nobles, sparked countless, varicoloured anecdotes that culminated in the events linked with Michelangelo and Julius II.

The Council of Trent, the foundation of the Jesuit Order, lead us to the 17th - 18th cent. and to new popes. The building and urban transformation they commissioned gave Rome distinctly Baroque tone.

Historic-religious events once again divided Latins and Germans and the formation of nations stressed the contrasts between the two worlds. Within the boundaries of the various states the Latin culture — Latin was the official language — adapted itself to the needs of each people. Though it was modified by contacts with local traditions, and at times seemed to disappear with the affirmation of aboriginal elements, it constituted in reality the most obvious characteristic and the principal note of progress. To this day, one can distinguish those nations which at some time or other felt the effects of Latin civilization, from the others.

The most outstanding feature in the field of urban development was the attention given by architects to the space around a building; and that explains those scenographical works: St. Peter's, Piazza di Spagna, Piazza del Quirinale, Piazza dell'Esquilino.

The people added background to the colourful entrances of new ambassadors; expressed their opinion through Pasquino and the talking statues; were debased by the games at Agone and Testaccio and the splendid carnivals of the Corso. After these diversions of ever vulgar taste, the sight of hanged and quartered bodies on streetcorners seemed quite natural. For a few centuries the population seemed to stagnate in this condition of servility.

With the French Revolution and Napoleon, the Jacobin turbulence was felt in Rome with the exile of the pope and the Peace of Tolentino. The subsequent reaction served only to heighten the Italian nationalistic movement which recognised its hero in Garibaldi and its enemy in the French, the upholders of temporal power.

Italy conquered Rome in 1870 and from then on the city underwent those transformations caused chiefly by an increase in population and its new status as capital. Thus a quarter in Piedmont style sprang up about Piazza Vittorio Emanuele II and, at the beginning of the new century, the grey structures around Via Vittorio Veneto were built on the demolished Villa Ludovisi. The former introduced the porticoed square and a grid of straight thoroughfares intersecting at right angles; the latter are heavy, showy buildings, originating from a middle class aspiring to nobility as the ideal state of existence. This is the so called Humbertan Rome, from the name of the king under whom the style flourished.

Following World War I and during the 20-year Fascist Regime, an architecture rich with marbles and statues tended to link itself with the most obvious manifestations of Roman greatness. The Foro Italico, the urban layout of Piazza Augusto Imperatore and the Imperial Forums, the E.U.R. zone were carried out while extensive archeological excavations were made. Population was on the increase; buildings rose more and more thickly on the Tiber's right bank, in the Prati di Castello and Monteverde quarters; and outside the walls, in S. Giovanni and S. Lorenzo. This expansion beyond the walls was further accentuated after World War II when the city counted a population of two million.

Currently the city offers many aspects: a central nucleus mainly comprised of ruins; a Renaissance zone facing St. Peter's on the opposite side of the river, where narrow streets and the houses with their steep staircases lend an air of fascination; the baroque and romantic zone clinging to the slopes of the Pincian and Quirinal and winding toward the Esquiline; the 19th century streets; those zones well-defined by recent history, and others toward the Salaria, Nomentana, Tiburtina, Casilina, Ostiense, which stress the hurried, chaotic development of present days. Representing the ruins and monuments, Rome's tradition of antiquity and the urban centres formed during successive periods of civilization make the city's adaptation to modern life an enormous problem.

Nevertheless, heavy traffic has been channelled, by means of countless one-way streets toward specific approaches terminating at the circular motorway 20 Km. away. It leads the driver to the various directions of the Autostrada del Sole. Well-defined laws serve to call a halt to unlimited urban development tending naturally toward the sea; and to regulate excavations still far from completion. Rome and its territory are indeed an inexhaustible mine of archeological treasures which aid in broadening our understanding of world civilization.

Rome's part in history is yet unfinished, not only for the information new finds can give up, but mainly for the continuous work of the papacy which today sends out its appeal to the ends of the earth and represents a stronghold of equilibrium in material events and a light of hope for the spiritual world.

Roman Countryside. Aqueduct, Ruins

Piazza S. Pietro

The Vatican. Piazza S. Pietro and Basilica.
Sistine Chapel - The Raphael Rooms - The Belvedere Court -
Vatican Museum and Picture Gallery.
Castel S. Angelo - Foro Italico - Trastevere - Janiculum

THE VATICAN

Located on the right bank of the Tiber the centre of Christianity occupies the former site of the ancient Vatican zone — hence the name — where Nero's garden and Circus were, and extends all the way to the Janiculum. There it is defended by fortifications (Leo IV, 847), and limited on either side by Borgo S. Spirito and the Passetto with S. Angelo. Along the central axis — v. della Conciliazione, St. Peter's and Piazza S. Pietro — buildings and gardens, squares and avenues are arranged in a vast urban complex where state services operate. The Basilica together with the Piazza is the centre and idealistic pivot of the church. Before it extend the borghi (burghs), which in the course of centuries underwent considerable transformations though all the while remaining overpopulated. The ample space in v. della Conciliazione seems to extend to humanity the ancient exchange of brotherly love.

Piazza S. Pietro.

(340×240 m.) is G. L. Bernini's masterpiece. The stupendous Colonnade — 284 columns, 88 pilasters, 140 statues — together with the Fountain to the left were completed under Alexander VII (1655—67). The other Fountain was erected by C. Maderno, the Obelisk is by C. Fontana (Sixtus V) who completed the work in 4 months using 44 winches, 900 workers and 140 horses. The 25.50 m. **Obelisk** resting on 4 bronze lions was transported from Heliopolis (Egypt) in the year 37 during the reign of Caligula, and used as a goal post in Nero's Circus; in Mediaeval times it was to be seen flanking the ancient basilica. It was then common belief that the ashes of Caesar were contained in the apex — Aguglia —; it now holds a relic of the Cross. Important is the depth it lends to the piazza and the manner in which it coordinates all of the single parts. The arrangement of the space before St. Peter's solved the problem created by Maderno's 3 - aisled prolongation of the basilica: the linking of St. Peter's to Rome. The square, laid out like the ruins of the Forum Augusti, widens to receive humanity in its generous embrace.

The Basilica.

Bramante's project — a central plan —, slightly modified by Michelangelo, had already solved the problem. St. Peter's should have stood alone, surrounded by a vast piazza, and have expressed a nearly metaphysical sense of isolation. Rome would have looked to it as to a source of light. Let

Piazza S. Pietro. G. Lorenzo Bernini: Colonnade (Detail)

each one judge which solution would have been the better; now, certainly, the **Façade** of St. Peter's (Maderno, 1607—14) reduces the impetus of Michelangelo's cupola.

On the central balcony or Papal Loggia, the new pope is presented to the people and receives the symbolical confirmation of his election. The statues of the Redeemer, the Baptist and the Apostles (5.70 m.) testify with the New Testament to a way of life based on love.

At the **Portico** (Maderno), 71×13×20 m., one steps into an area of well-defined concepts represented by the statues at the extremities: Constantine (Bernini, 1670), Charlemagne (Cornacchini, 1725). Constantine with the Edict of 313 conferred on Christianity the same rights enjoyed by other religions; Charlemagne, in submitting to his investiture with the dignity of emperor at the hands of Leo III (St. Peter's, Christmas 800), acknowledged the pope and the Roman people as the holders of such authority. The door to the far right is the Holy Door, opened only during Jubilee years. The bronze Central Door was cast by A. Filarete (1433-45) and represents Rome's first Renaissance work.

Scenes of religious character — Christ, the Virgin, St. Peter — follow others of classical derivation — Leda and the Swan, the She-wolf, heads of emperors — and those relating specifically to the life of Pope Eugenius IV. But neither the mythological sensualism nor the boastfulness of the sculptor — Self Portrait — arrive at raising the work above a level of purely technical perfection or at reducing the dryness of detail. Of high artistic value is Manzu's ten-panelled. **Door of Death,** to the left.

The interior is an immense space — 186 m. long, covering a surface of 15,160 sq. m. — in the form of a Latin cross with chapels ordered in a manner typical of churches of the Counter Reformation. It is covered with gold, stuccoes, projecting cornices, statues (18th cent.) that all but move within their niches. The various parts attain uncommon measures as if the regulating concept had been that of surpassing human limits; nonetheless, they are organized according to strict rules of proportion. The « grand manner » arrangement achieved with the refined intuitiveness of the Renaissance costitutes the originality of this architecture.

Having absorbed these various impressions, we walk down the central nave letting memories come to mind. Here, in this space, those recollections come alive: Palestine and Greece, Egypt and the Orient; Rome, Christ; Peter and Paul; Nero and Caligula; the catacombs and the martyrs; down the centuries to John XXIII, Paul VI and Vatican II.

The statue of St. Peter — last pilaster to the right — merits the utmost attention. According to tradition Arnolfo di Cambio (1298) moulded it with the bronze taken from the statue of Capitoline Jupiter. The sculptor modelled St. Peter with a classic head — hair, beard, eyes — and in a seated position, the body compact under an ample robe the few folds of which are ordered in classic pattern.

The arms and hands, that could dominate an assembly, clasp the keys and confer a blessing. Humanity pauses to kiss the foot, wearing it away, and waits: while on Peter and the Church, expressed most clearly in this statue, weighs the burden of eternity. In the transept rise the dark columns of the baldachin, which attracts the eye from the time one enters; and around it is the great space created by Michelangelo. It is limited by pilasters which support the drum and accentuated in the immensity of the Cupola — diam. 42 m., ht. 132.50 m. —. Here is an example of the complete domination of space, in the manner of the ancient Romans, and before such power the observer feels perplexed and even stunned. The cupola is in two shells recalling the Pantheon and Florence's Baptistery and S. Maria del Fiore, only that here rigid Florentine logic is developed along monumental lines and brought to its maximum perfection.

Bernini's bronze **Baldachin** (canopy), 29 m. high and as tall as Palazzo Farnese, was cast from bronze beams removed from the Pantheon (1624—33) by order of Urban VIII. Following this new outrage on antiquity, the pope was frankly criticized by Pasquino « Quod non fecerunt Barbari, fecerunt Barberini » and the saying has survived the centuries. The baldachin covers an Altar where only the Pope may say Mass. Below it is the burial-vault where the relics of St. Peter are kept and before which is the kneeling statue of Pius VI (marble, Canova).

We return to the main door. Set in the pavement is a red porphyry disk once located near the high altar. Charlemagne and other emperors knelt on it at coronations. In the first chapel to the right is Michelangelo's marble group, the **Pietà** (1499—1500).

The 25 - year - old Michelangelo had been in Rome only a short time (1496) when he began to sculpture the group for Card. de la Grolaie. Both in Florence and here he nourished a keen sense of rebellion and criticism against the vice and mysticism, the crimes and follies that characterized the times.

The Pietà originated from this spiritual stand. A pyramidal composition comprising the Mother — base and vertex — and the Son laid across her lap, it expresses a mother's grief for her dead son. The work is a result of contrasts — vertical mother, transversal son; the one clothed, the other naked; unreal folds and high polish — with the mother's face and hand in relief: the former touched by light where it eludes the shadow of the veil, the latter dropping into space in seeming despair. In the immobility of the facial muscles the mother reflects an almost abstract grief which becomes universal sorrow. In the third bay opens the Chapel of the Sacrament with Bernini's Ciborium (1674) and the Trinity, an altarpiece by Pietro da Cortona. Beyond the monument to Gregory XIII, the pope who reformed the calendar (1582), is the square area (perimeter, 71 m.) created by Michelangelo with its piers. A few columns from the ancient basilica have been arranged in the chapels at the adjacent corners. Across the transept is the monument to Clement XIII (Canova, 1788—92).

At the end of the apse is the **Chair** (Bernini, 1656—65), a baroque composition of apparent symbolism supported by the Doctors of the Church, Ambrose and Augustine, Athanasius and John Chrysostom, who constitute the pillars of its doctrine. It encloses a wooden one where Peter supposedly sat. On the right is the monument to Urban VIII Barberini (Bernini, 1642—47) with the bees of his escutcheon lighting here and there and vanishing before death. To the left, the monument to Paul III Farnese (G. della Porta, 1551—75) is decorated with the statues of Justice, a portrait of his sister Julia, and Prudence, that of his mother Giovanella Caetani. The third, della Colonna Chapel, contains the altarpiece, St. Leo encounters Attila (A. Algardi), and also the tombs of Popes Leo II, III, IV and, in the centre, that of Leo XII. Beyond the transept is the entrance to the

Sacristy.

It is a building in itself (18th cent.). Just past the entrance is a marble inscription listing the names of the 144 popes entombed in the basilica. In the octagonal Sagrestia Comune are 8 grey columns — from the Villa of Hadrian —; a bronze cock (9th cent.) that once adorned the campanile of the ancient basilica, an obvious allusion to Christ's words to Peter, « Before the cock crows thou shalt deny me thrice ». Donatello's Ciborium (1432) and a panel depicting the Madonna della Febbre may be found to the right in the Beneficiati Sacristy. Next is the

Treasury,

sacked for the last time during the Peace of Tolentino (1797). Striking are the richness of the vestments and the perfection of the various objects among which: the ring of Sixtus IV; the cross of Emperor Justin II; a dalmatic of the 10th or 11th cent.; two candelabra by Pollaiuolo. We proceed to the Clementine Chapel where, below the altar, are the remains of St. Gregory. Past the Chapel of the Choir is the tomb of Innocent VIII (A. Pollaiuolo, 1498), the only monument transferred here from the old basilica. Below the monument to M. C. Sobieski is the passage to the

Cupola.

The balcony affords a splendid view of the piazza and the 92 m. cupola. 537 stairs lead to the high balcony around the lantern where one may admire a panorama of the Vatican gardens and the city.

The Vatican Grottoes

(Entrance: left side of basilica).

Located on a level between the present basilica and the Constantinian one, the grottoes, through relics still preserved there, provide a link between the two. Tombstones and a monument to Sixtus IV by A. Pollaiuolo (1493), one of the most typical works of the early Renaissance, may be seen in the 6 rooms forming the entrance wing. A passageway in the third room leads down to the pagan-christian necropolis upon which the ancient basilica was built.

Vatican. Sistine Chapel

The Old Grottoes (Paul V, 1606) possess precious tomb-stones, busts, inscriptions, recording a few popes buried in the old basilica — Boniface VIII, Innocent VII — and Emperor Otto II. A few chapels excavated in the New Grottoes (1534—1546) preserve remains of the monument to Paul II (G. Dàlmata and Mino da Fiésole, 1471), statues and, in the Chapel of St. Peter, a 4th cent. altar. A similar wealth of ancient elements may be seen in the exit wing, where outstanding is the sarcophagus of Junius Bassus (4th cent.) covered with delicate sculptures and symbolical figures.

VATICAN MUSEUM AND PICTURE GALLERY

(For greater detail catalogues listing all the works may be obtained here.)

The 17 - room painting display offers a precious panorama of the schools of painting from the primitives to the moderns. Room I, of the Primitives: contains the most ancient work of the collection, Last Judgement, 526 (9th cent.); in the middle: the Cope of Boniface VIII, an English embroidery (13th cent.). Room II is renowned for the Stefaneschi polyptych by Giotto, 120. Christ's majestic bearing reveals a classical tradition, and the position of the angels is an essay at spatial effects. There are also works by Ambrogio and Pietro Lorenzetti, L. Monaco, Vecchietta and Sassetta. The Florentine tradition continues in Room III with paintings by B. Angelico, F. Lippi and B. Gozzoli who illustrate the setting and atmosphere of 15th cent. Florence. Room IV is known as the room of Melozzo da Forlì owing to painting 270, showing the investiture of Platina as librarian to the pope. The fresco transferred onto canvas, is famous for its portraits: Sixtus IV, seated, Platina kneeling, and between them Card. Giuliano della Rovere, the future Julius II. The figures are arranged in space with the same values of monumentality as may be seen in architecture and seem to represent a high civilization. We cross rooms V, VI, VII to Room VIII where some of Raphael's works are displayed: 10 Tapestries — 7 of the original cartoons may be found at the Victoria and Albert Museum in London —, the Madonna di Foligno (1512—13) and the Transfiguration. The Tapestries, woven for the lower walls of the Sistine Chapel (Brussels, Van Aelst), represent the following scenes: the blinding of Elymas — cut during the Sack —, the conversion of St. Paul, the Stoning of St. Stephen, St. Peter heals the lame man, the Death of Ananias, Christ giving the keys to Peter, the Miraculous draught of fishes, St. Paul preaching at Athens, the Sacrifice at Lystra, St. Paul in prison; and are admirable for the precious workmanship which in no way diminishes the vivacity of design or delicacy of colour. The **Transfiguration** (1517), completed in the lower portion by G. Romano with heavy, rhetorical figures, was placed at the head of Raphael's bier. In the scene comprising a mountain entoured by trees and half dissolved in light, like Christ and the Prophets, the essence of the miraculous event is expressed with delicacy of touch and a sensitivity to colour.

Room IX is noteworthy for the monochrome, St. Jerome, by Leonardo. The figure of the penitent, consumed with intense spirituality, solitary against a rocky landscape and horrid background, is profoundly inspiring.

Works of the Venetian school are displayed in Room X; outstanding among them is Titian's Madonna of S. Nicolò dei Frari, 351. The warm, luminous colours laid in strata on the canvas express a mature reality, and the figures are wrapped in a hazy, tactile atmosphere. Room XII contains Domenichino's most famous work, Last Communion of St. Jerome. The Entombment scene (Caravaggio, 1602—04) takes place in an atmosphere of intense drama mainly due to the focusing of the composition on the illuminated body of Christ, while figures round about, in various tragic poses, emerge from the shadows.

We cross the remaining rooms to the Porch of the Four Doors and go up left to the **Egyptian** Museum (Pius VII, 19 th cent.), arranged opposite the Borgia apartment: these halls contain sarcophagi, statues and other objects sacred to the cult of the dead. Having reached the semicircle we pass through the doorway facing showcase 217 — apply to the guardian — and exit into the Courtyard of the Pigna with its apse by P. Ligorio. This vast area, originally known as the Belvedere Court was first obstructed by the construction of the Library wing (Sixtus V) and then by the New Wing, so that it is now divided into three parts known as the Courts of Belvedere, the Library and, at the far side, Pigna.

A few decorative works have been arranged on the framing of the apse. The Pigna, a fountain in the shape of a pine cone, subsequently gave its name to the entire court area and is the symbol of one of Rome's districts. Dante glimpsed it in the narthex of old St. Peter's where it then served a decorative function. The well-formed Capital (3rd cent.) originates from the Alexandrian Thermae; the refined Peacocks were discovered in the Tomb of Hadrian.

We return to Room I and enter the **Pio-Clementine** Museum where original statues and copies of 1st and 2nd cent. works may be found. The interesting collection with its wealth of sculpture, sarcophagi and mosaics is arranged in 18th cent. settings.

The rooms take their names either from their shape or from the specific works they contain. In the Hall of the Greek Cross one may admire two works famous for the people for whom they were destined: 566 and 598, the sarcophagi of Ss. Costance and Helen. We cross the Round Hall, Hall of the Muses, of the Animals. The Room of the Busts is situated in a wing of the small palace of the Belvedere (Innocent VIII, 1487). Worthy of mention are: 264, Apollo slaying the lizard, from a bronze original by Praxiteles; 250, Eros of Centocelle, from an original of the 4th cent. B. C. The busts of a sullen Caracalla and, 273, of Octavian as a youth, are interesting.

We cross the gallery of the busts and enter the Cabinet of the **Masks** — if closed apply to the guardian — the name of which is derived from the subject of the fine mosaics removed from the Villa of Hadrian. Very important is the Venus of Cnidos (474), a replica of Praxiteles' 4th cent. B. C. masterpiece. If open, step onto the open Loggia. This construction is very interesting, not only for the works it contains but above all because it encloses the Octagonal court, world-famous as the **Belvedere** — two courtyards bear this name — where marvellous sculptures are on display; the Laocoön, Hermes, Perseus, Apollo, and, in a separate room, the Torso. The courtyard is reached from the Hall of the Animals.

The **Laocoön** — right — is a Greek marble group, discovered in Nero's Golden House (1506), signed by the Rhodian sculptors Agesander, Athenodorus, Polydorus (1st cent. B. C.). It represents a father and his two sons gripped by serpents and recalls the episode of the horse drawn before Troy and of the priest Laocoön urging his fellow citizens to destroy it prophesying impending ruin to the city. Two serpents sprang from the sea, reached Laocoön and his sons before the temple and suffocated them in their coils.

The famous group reaches its climax in the son to the left, crying for help and knowing full well the futility of it.

The Apollo Belvedere discovered at Grottaferrata in the 15th cent. is a marble copy of an original 4th cent. bronze. Captivating is the serenity of the god as he watches the flight of an arrow he has just shot, and his physical beauty.

After the Perseus, sculptured by Canova, and the Hermes, copy of a 4th cent. B. C. original, through the doorway on the wall between Perseus and Apollo we reach the Round Hall and the admirable **Apoxyomenos,** an athlete scraping himself with a strigil. It is a copy of a bronze by Lysippus, 4th cent. B. C., existent in Rome during Pliny's times and retrieved from the Tiber in the 19th cent.

Following — to the left — is the stairway by Bramante (16th cent.) built into the corner tower of Belvedere, and from the window one can view the fountain of the Galley in the gardens. Across the Round Room is the Room of the **Torso.** The armless marble, the legs truncated, represents a person seated on the skin of a wild beast. The form and muscles display power and virility: it appears to be a Hercules. The work, found in the 15th cent., bears the signature of the Athenian, Apollonius of Nestor.

We go down the main staircase to the Chiaramonti Gallery. The 300 m. long gallery links the small palace of Innocent VIII with the Vatican palace. Canova suggested the arrangement of statues, sarcophagi and hermae that constitute the Chiaramonti and Inscription Galleries and the New Wing.

The Inscription Gallery — admittance by special permit — contains over 5000 Christian and pagan inscriptions. To the right, on the other hand, one may enter the New Wing, 70×80 m., where famous works have been set out, outstanding among which is **Augustus,** found in the 19th cent. at Prima Porta in the Villa of Livia. The statue shows Augustus, with sceptre and cuirass, and about to speak. Note the scene on the breastplate depicting the Parthian king, Phraates,

Vatican, Borgia Apartment. Pinturicchio: Portrait of Lucretia Borgia

restoring to Tiberius the Roman standards lost by Crassus. The emperor's serious determined face expresses authority, and the wide sweep of the hand echoes a distinct state of mind. It portrays Augustus at the height of his power, a true symbol of the empire. Moreover, statues of Nile (106), a Hellenistic work and of the Doryphorus, a replica of a 5th cent. B. C. bronze by Polyclitus may be seen. At the end we turn right and return to the entrance of the Gallery. The first room is the Museum of Pagan Antiquities — overlooking the Pigna Courtyard — in an 18th cent. setting (Clement XIII and Pius IV) with furniture by L. Valadier.

The **Clementine Gallery,** which follows, is important for its collection of Maps of Rome (apply to the secretary's office). After the Alexandrine and Pauline Rooms we turn left to the Sistine Hall 70×16 m. (D. Fontana, 1587—89) with cross vault and pilasters. Interesting are the Views of Rome with the various transformations brought about by Sixtus V. The Gallery of Urban VIII follows. Next is the Museum of Christian Art located alongside the Borgia apartments, where Christian antiquities are displayed (Benedict XIV, 1756). Very important is the Hall of the **Aldobrandini Wedding,** probably a reproduction of a fresco by Aëtion painted during the times of Alexander the Great, which depicts the wedding of this King to Roxana (Esquiline, 1605). Moreover, other frescoes illustrate: landscapes of the Odyssey; the heroine of Tor Marancia; a Children's Procession; laden Cargo Boats. Now we enter the

Borgia Apartments located lengthwise between the Courtyards of Belvedere and Pappagalli. Six rooms comprise them and they are best known as the residence of Alexander VI and for the fresco cycle by Pinturicchio (1492—95). Here dwelled Caesar Borgia, his sister Lucretia, Giulia Farnese and Vanozza, Micheletto, protagonists of an epoch over which history prefers to draw a veil of silence while literature holds them responsible for even the most dreadful crimes — murder of the Duke of Candia — and abnormal vices. The paintings convey a faint echo of those events. In Room IV the frescoes achieve a high artistic level while tapestries and furniture create a 15th cent. environment. The religious scenes, events from the lives of the Saints: Paul the Hermit and Anthony the Monk, Catherine and Barbara, chaste Susanna and Sebastian, portray actual personages of the times; and together with others of paganistic character — Isis, Osiris, Io — they reflect that period. Similar in decoration are the following rooms. Returning, we walk down to the

SISTINE CHAPEL

(Sixtus IV. G. Dei Dolci, 1473—84).

It is a spacious area — 40.50×13.20×20.70 m. — uninterrupted by columns, enclosed by walls with arched windows and topped by a barrel vault; bare; and the final result is one of severity, of near coldness. This hall is used for the election of the pope — the conclave is held here — and constitutes a setting preparatory to the church. The pavement is 15th cent. and the carvings were accomplished by Mino da Fiésole — screen —, A. Bregno and G. Dàlmata. The Sistine is celebrated for its frescoes.

The six scenes depicted on each wall (1481—83) narrate, to the left, episodes from the life of Moses, the prophet-sustainer of the Old Testament, and, to the right, Jesus, founder of the New. Following in sequence are: The journey of Moses into Egypt (Pinturicchio); Moses and the Daughters of Jethro (Botticelli), animated by a fine poetical sentiment; Crossing of the Red Sea, Moses and the Tablets by C. Rosselli; the Destruction of the sons of Korah is descriptively interesting owing to the background scene with the Arch of Constantine and the Septizonium now destroyed and the portrait of the youth — later Paul III — and of Pomponio Leto, the famous man of letters, holding him by the hand.

The Death of Moses by L. Signorelli is highly esteemed and Michelangelo here seems to have drawn inspiration for the Nudes of the vault. Following are: Baptism of Jesus (Pinturicchio). In the Temptation of Jesus, by Botticelli, the temple in the background is the Hospital of S. Spirito. Next, the Calling of the Apostles (D. Ghirlandaio); the Sermon on the Mount (C. Rosselli and Piero di Cosimo); the Giving of the keys to Peter, by Perugino, and the Last Supper, by C. Rosselli. Some of these scenes are noteworthy for their backgrounds of imaginary architecture, others for their refined compositions; all together they constitute the most complete painting cycle of the 15th cent. Between the windows appear the first 28 popes, painted by Ghirlandaio and Botticelli.

The Sistine Ceiling

By order of Julius II, Michelangelo frescoed the 800 metre vault (1508—12) subjecting himself to a gruelling task which produced in him those fits of temper so colourfully recorded in literary anecdotes. He accomplished a work welded by poetical sentiment and technical perfection synthesizing inspiration with plastic figures in the round, that still remain a standard of art. The nine scenes along the central field narrate scenes from Genesis and are known as Michelangelo's Bible. They are — from the door to the Judgement — in the order in which Michelangelo painted them — the Drunkenness of Noah and the Deluge. Notable is the lack of technical expression. The Sacrifice of Noah, Temptation and Expulsion. Full of desperation, Adam and Eve's bearing carries the imprint of Masaccio. Creation of Adam and Eve is the most notable episode both for the formal perfection — according to Goethe, Adam comes closer than any other figure to pure physical beauty —, and the spiritual intensity, which animates God and Adam. Evident is the sense of fatigue which characterizes Adam as though the spark of life transmitted by the Creator — the two fingers! — had summoned him from unknown distances. Separation of the waters from the earth, Creation of fishes, sun, moon, plants. The dividing of light from darkness. The corners of each scene are filled with Nudes and along the lateral spaces, with Prophets and Sibyls alternately. The Delphic Sibyl — at the start, right — and

Vatican, Sistine Chapel, Vault.
Michelangelo Buonarroti: Frescoes (Detail) ➜

Jeremiah — left, end — surpass all others for spirit and individuality of character.

Last Judgement

Commissioned by Paul III (1534—41), Michelangelo's fresco depicts an apocalyptical vision of a scene whose desperate protagonist is mankind. The contrasts of the first decades of the century had left their mark on Michelangelo's spirit so that the vision of classic beauty yielded, with the approach of death, to considerations of moral force. In these scenes he poured that particular atmosphere of the times, painting as though tides of violence and calumny were crowding his spirit, pushing him ahead at a breathless pace.

He based the composition on Christ and developed the theme on those lines which divide the human from the supernatural. Christ's humanity is cancelled by the light and shade that underscore the act from which Christ neither can — concept of Fate — nor wishes to escape. The presence of the timid Mother lends added force to this impression.

The multiple variations of Vice and Virtue that comprise mankind fall into their places in a series of instinctive gestures, which light and shadow crystallize in eternal distinction: The Offering of the Instruments of Martyrdom, a terrorized figure staring wide eyed, Charon, Minos — a portrait of Biagio da Cesena, Paul III's master of ceremonies —, the Damned grasping at the Elect, the Angels banishing the Damned. An ancestral dread and the movement that subjects forms to action and sentiment, the infernal shrieking of trumpets that conquer death, dominate the scene before which the spirit recoils in terror.

Through the doorway at the end, to the right of the altar, we go up to the

RAPHAEL ROOMS (STANZE)

situated above the Borgia apartments.

Raphael, summoned to Rome by Julius II, painted the **Signatura** Room (1508 - 1511), the fourth from the entrance; the name is derived from a tribunal. The pavement was laid in the 15th cent.

The Disputa covers the entrance wall. This is the first fresco Raphael completed in Rome. We see: on high, God the Father; in the centre, Christ, the Virgin and the Baptist; along the sides Patriarchs, Apostles, symbols of the Old and New Testaments. Below, representatives of religion discuss (disputa), read and pray about the Host placed on the altar: St. Gregory the Great and Savonarola; B. Angelico and Ss. Jerome, Ambrose and Augustine; Dante and St. Thomas; solitary or grouped, timid or self-assured according to the character of each. The various parts are achieved in idealogical perfection. These events are expressed with the utmost freedom and the characters are grouped heedless of historical dates: Umbrian tradition dominates scene, characters, treatment of robes, hair and expressions; while the poses of some of the personages show the influence of Rome: the statuesque figure to the left and the pope opposite. Here, Raphael reveals himself as painter-personifier of the essence of Christian art.

The Triumph of Philosophy may be seen on the opposite wall in the

School of Athens.

The fresco, under a vault of noble architecture, shows separate groups of men whose common interest centres on the two central figures: Plato (a portrait of Leonardo da Vinci) pointing upward and holding his book, the Timaeus; Aristotle, gesturing boldly toward the earth and holding his Ethics.

On these two creators of thought is focused the attention of the others, each in his own characteristic manner: Diogenes, sprawled and half-dressed, turns a shoulder; Heraclitus, a portrait of Michelangelo, seated, head in hand; Socrates counting the syllogisms on his fingers; F. Maria della Rovere in a white mantle to the left, behind Anaxagoras holding a book. On the opposite side to the right is the portrait of Raphael, the young man wearing a black beret.

Raphael painted the fresco in 1509 when the Umbrian influence had by then ceded to monumentality of design, arrangement, setting, and to figures of a classic order. Here, poetical purity enhances everything and culture is represented in a superb manner.

To the right is the **Glorification of Justice** — ceiling — depicting Virtues and the Laws. The last painting in the room — opposite wall — is the Glorification of Poetry in the

Parnassus (1511).

The subject lends itself to Raphael's own lyrical character; a subtle aura pervades the faces and attitudes of Apollo and the Muses, intent on hearing him. Then follow poets clearly defined: Homer, Virgil, Dante, Ennius, Sappho; and Ariosto, Ovid and others. The figure of Calliope, the body compact under the loosened white gown, is of such classic beauty as to be considered a Venus.

In this room, Raphael's art reaches its climax and it is here that he acquired fame and fortune: in Roman circles he was so sought after that he no longer had time to paint; thus from this moment, with a few exceptions, his work was limited to cartoons and the retouching of executions by others. The frescoes of the **Heliodorus Room,** following, (1512—14) are indicative of the change in papacy from Julius II to Leo X and of the beginning of those works carried out mainly by his assistants. On the entrance wall one can view Leo I — Leo X — turning back Attila, by G. Romano and F. Penni. Opposite is the Expulsion of Heliodorus, who has fallen to the ground with a vase of coins stolen from the temple of Jerusalem. Noteworthy — to the left — are the portraits of Julius II and Raphael, standing next to the pope. Following — left wall — is the Liberation of Peter, a fresco renowned for its treatment of light — moon, torches, angel —; and was in fact completed by the master himself. **The Miracle at Bolsena** — opposite wall — is outstanding; Raphael assimilated colour from the Venetian school, represented in Rome by Sebastiano del Piombo (1511), and used it with finesse and mastery — 5 sediarii, bearers of the pope's processional litter, lower right, and the portraits of Julius II, Card. R. Riario, right, and Card. di S. Giorgio, left —. This is Raphael's last work in the Stanze.

We return to Room II, painted by G. Romano and F. Penni between 1514—17. The ceiling was decorated by Perugino in 1508. Events which took place during the reign of Leo III, Coronation of Charlemagne, may be found on the entrance wall; of Leo IV opposite; and of Leo III at the far side. The **Fire in the Borgo** is important for a view of the façade of the ancient basilica and because the episode with the group of Aeneas becomes a classic event. One may note that Mannerism had its origins here.

We cross back through the two rooms and enter Room IV decorated with frescoes by F. Penni, G. Romano and others, that narrate facts from the life of Constantine. At the end begin the Logge planned by Bramante and Raphael (1512—18), and decorated with frescoes illustrating events from the New Testament —·12 bays — and from the Old — 13th bay — which constitute ·Raphael's Bible. « Grotesque » decoration, which the painters now discover (F. Penni, G. Romano, Perin del Vaga), is here used for the first time. From the Logge through the Chiaroscuro-Squires Room one reaches the **Chapel of St. Nicholas** where B. Angelico (1447—49) frescoed events from the lives of St. Lawrence, — Sixtus II is a portrait of Nicholas V — and, above, of St. Stephen, manifesting once again the serene essence of his faith.

We return to the Room of the Fire in the Borgo. From here we may reach the chapel of Urban VIII decorated by Pietro da Cortona. To the right we enter the Hall of the Immaculate Conception (19th cent.). Other halls follow and form the gallery of Modern Painting. In the Delle Dame Hall — end — the ceiling frescoes are by G. Reni (1575—1642). Following are: Gallery of the Geographical Maps (I. Danti, 1580—83); Gallery of the Tapestries where the originals from cartoons by Raphael were conserved. The present ones belong to the new series and were woven by the same factory. Next is the Gallery of the Candelabra with 19th cent. decorations. Noteworthy are (V) 5, Running Girl, a replica of the 5th cent. B.C. bronze original in archaic style; (IV) 66, Girl and a Goose, copy of a bronze by Boethus of Chalcedon (3rd cent. B.C.); (III) 12, mosaic of the 2nd cent.; (II) 42 and 51, two pairs of Candelabra — hence the name of the Room — originate from S. Costanza and S. Agnese; 32 and 39, two pairs of candelabra from Otricoli (2nd cent.). To the left we enter the Hall of the **Biga,** called after the superb chariot (2nd cent.) the central part of which was once used as an episcopal throne in St. Mark's. The Hall is decorated in a typical 17th cent. manner. The statues belong to the 5th, 4th, 3rd cent. B.C. Returning, we may go up to the **Gregorian-**

Etruscan Museum (Gregory XVI, 1837), with decorations of the 16th cent., located on the opposite side of Raphael's Stanze. Besides the various bronze objects from tombs, there is a bronze statue in Room III of **Mars of Todi** (5th cent. B. C.). Now we cross the other rooms for a complete view of the whole.

We return to Piazza S. Pietro and enter v. della Conciliazione. To the left, half way up, rises Palazzo Torlonia and farther ahead the church of S. Maria in Traspontina. In the 3rd chapel to the left are the columns to which Ss. Peter and Paul are supposed to have been bound. At the end to the left we reach

Castel S. Angelo.

Built as a mausoleum by Hadrian between 135 and 139, it comprised a cella for urns with a spiral ramp and a gallery; the exterior had a square base, a central cylinder covered with earth where pine trees grew and was surmounted by a chariot with the statue of Hadrian in the form of the sun (Helios). An approach, the nearby bridge, was built. In 271 Aurelian converted it into a fortified bastion; during the first invasions it became a fortress against whose walls and under whose fragmented statues, the Goths met destruction; it subsequently became a papal stronghold.

Reconstructed, it was adapted for use as a prison: Crescentius was hanged from its battlements, Cardinal Vitelleschi was strangled (1440) and Stefano Porcari met the same end. In Renaissance times it reached maximum notoriety involving such personages as Cellini and Clement VII. Card. Carafa, the Cenci and Giordano Bruno. The castle was used as a prison until the beginning of the 20th cent.

The present construction comprises a quadrangular wall fortified at the corners by four bastions — Ss. Matthew, John, Luke, Mark —, a cylindrical body, the machicolations of which were added by order of Alexander VI, and upon this rises the transversal wing, where the loggia of Julius II is located, a terrace and the Angel. Down the centuries the interior was transformed and adapted to the needs of the times; at present it preserves the cylindrical nucleus and central tower of the Roman epoch; many of the rooms are reconstructed settings of past centuries while others contain various collections.

Just inside, downstairs — Room 1; follow the numbers —, plastic models illustrate the most important changes in the castle through the centuries. The spiral ramp with its remnants of Roman pavement opens onto the dreadful prisons among which is Sammalo, the most notorious, where Cellini was committed. Another ramp, built under Alexander VI leads to the drawbridge above the cella, where the urns were, and finally, to the Delle Palle Courtyard. The narrow space is occupied by piles of cannon balls — hence the name — and in the rooms all around one can glimpse settings of the past like the 16th cent. guard-room.

Beyond the door to the left, the Hall of Justice — Roman —, and of Apollo (Paul III, 1547), at the end to the right is the

45

admirable Chapel of Leo X. Through the Halls of Clement VII we exit into the Courtyard of Alexander VI, where there is the entrance, right, down to the historic prisons, while round about are the cells once used for important personalities.

We go up to the Loggia of Julius II overlooking the Elio Bridge. Then we enter the apartments of Paul III, formed by the Hall, the Rooms of Perseus, Eros and Psyche. These rooms are interesting for their frescoes (Perin del Vaga and Baccio da Montelupo), statues, furniture (16th cent.) and tapestries which conjure up a specific atmosphere. The Library follows, and is decorated with remarkable stuccoes and frescoes as are the two adjacent rooms — Hadrianian and Festoon —, sometimes closed to the public. The door to the right opens onto the Roman room known as the Treasury, where coffers are kept. We reach the Terrace by means of the stairway — marvellous panorama! —. Here one may see the Angel and the Bell of Mercy sounded only on occasions of capital punishment.

The Passetto is a high fortified passage linking the castle with the Vatican palace.

Along the Lungotevere to the left is the Palace of Justice (Calderini, 20th cent.). Behind it stretch the Prati di Castello, once fields belonging to Castel S. Angelo, where enemy hordes used to camp on their way to conquer Rome; it is now a residential area, still called Prati.

The zone is subdivided into numerous streets intersecting at right angles. At the level of the Matteotti Bridge, we turn left — Vle delle Milizie — and proceed to Lgo Trionfale; we take the second street to the right — v. Trionfale — and continue to Mte Mario — Panorama — for a visit to Villa Mellini, now an astronomical and meteorological Observatory as well as a Museum. We return by way of Ple Clodio and Pza Mlo Giardino; turn left — v. di Vla Madama — where Villa Madama rises (Raphael. 1516—17). We proceed to the **Foro Italico, a** zone for athletic games where the Olympic stadium is located — 100.000 spectators —, the Marble stadium with its beautiful statues of athletes and numerous gymnasiums.

Returning to v. della Conciliazione, halfway up to the left is Palazzo dei Penitenzieri (XV cent.). We turn left and reach Borgo S. Spirito where the Hospital and Church of S. Spirito in Sassia — corruption of Wessex — are located. Toward the year 1000 the zone was inhabited by citizens of various nationalities who constituted, around the 16th cent., a wealthy upper middle class. Its decline originated with the Sack when it gradually became a quarter for a more modest population.

Porta S. Spirito, a massive construction restricted by the bastions of Pius IV (1654) is well known for the fact that the Spaniards forced it during the famous siege that saw the death of the Prince of Bourbon.

After crossing Pza della Rovere, we take the Lungara — a straight street — opened by Julius II. At N. 10, is the Pzo Corsini (Fuga, 1732—36). It rises on the site of the former 15th cent. palace of Card. D. Riario, renowned during the times of Christina of Sweden, who here founded the Academy, forerunner of the Arcadia. It was also an attraction in the Napoleonic epoch.

The rooms on the first floor constitute the **National Gallery of Ancient Art** where paintings mainly of the 17th and 18th cent. are displayed. Outstanding are: Views, by G. P. Pannini, and Ruins, by A. Gaspari, which illustrate well-known though transformed landscapes. After the Still Lifes and scenes of Arcady is P. P. Rubens' St. Sebastian and the sweet, almost homely Madonna by Murillo in Room III; Venetian Views by Canaletto, all air and light, and Judith by G. B. Piazzetta. Beyond the Baptist by Caravaggio, characterized by contrasts of light and shadow, is the Crib by P. Batoni, enhanced by an original 18th cent. frame.

In the palace one may also visit the Odescalchi Collection of Arms.

Facing Palazzo Corsini — N. 230 — is the **Farnesina** (B. Peruzzi, 1508—11), probably the most renowned Renaissance villa.

It is an architectural and decorative jewel. The construction rises in balanced proportions in two projecting wings framing a façade with five arches and embellished with windows and an exquisite frieze of fruit and flowers. The interior possesses decorations by Raphael — Gallery: the Fable of Psyche, 1517; and room to the left: Galatea, 1511; by B. Peruzzi — first floor ceiling and room to the right; and by Sodoma — right hand room: Marriage of Alexander and Roxana, 1511—12 —, his masterpiece.

Agostino Chigi who had it built exercised considerable influence in Roman circles during the reigns of Alexander VI and Leo X. In fact, in this villa frequented by popes and princes, each had his own coat of arms engraved on the golden tableware which, at the end of each course, they cast into the Tiber; a hidden net preserved them. In the villa one may visit the **National Cabinet of Engravings.**

The Torlonia Museum — v. Corsini, 5 — houses a collection of ancient sculptures, among which an illustration of the port of Ostia. The Septimiana Gate, commissioned by Alexander VI, with a fornix and ghibelline merlons on machicolations, closes the Lungara. Beyond the gate to the left - v. S. Dorotea, 20 - is the house of the Fornarina immortalized by Raphael. We return to the gate and take v. S. Maria della Scala. We are now in the heart of Trastevere, a picturesque quarter whose inhabitants still claim to be representatives of the true Roman tradition. A wealth of literature gives prominence to this claim, which probably dates from very ancient times. In fact, during the Roman epoch this was the Etruscan zone whose population was given to soothsaying; and here the Jews had their first synagogue. The Trasteverini, following an ancestral vocation, later formed the backbone of the papal army. Nowadays, manifestations of their character may be seen in their processions.

Located in the centre of the region are Piazza and Basilica di **S. Maria in Trastevere.** This was the first church officially opened in Rome. The present complex boasts a façade and campanile of the 12th cent. Basilican in character, the interior comprises three aisles, 21 ancient columns, trabeations with remnants of Roman constructions. The most interesting parts are the pulpit (12th cent.) and the mosaics by P. Cavallini (13th cent.) in the apse; in the left aisle, mosaics of the Augustan period; the 12th - 13th cent. façade mosaics. Legend has it that oil gushed from a spot beneath the high altar, 37 B. C. foretelling the arrival of Christ.

We continue — left, front — to v. della Lungaretta and Piazza Sonnino characterized by the 12th cent. Degli Anguillara Tower and — right — the church of S. Crisognono with 12th cent. apse and campanile, and whose interior — three aisles, 21 columns and cosmatesque pavement — is basilican in character. Frescoes of the 8th and 9th cent. may be found on the subterranean level.

We cross Vle Trastevere and Pza in Piscinula — right — past v. Salumai and v. Genovesi where the church of **St. Cecilia** in Trastevere stands (Fuga, 1725; the decorative urn dates from antiquity). The building rises on the site of the house of St. Valerian, husband of Cecilia. She was put to death under Marcus Aurelius. Still to be seen is the room where vain attempts to suffocate her were made. Noteworthy are the frescoes (12th—13th cent.); flanking the apse, the Ciborium by Arnolfo di Cambio (1283); the statue of St. Cecilia (S. Maderno, 1600) on the high altar and the mosaic of the apse. From the crypt — apply to the guardian — we go down for a glimpse at the remnants of the Roman construction.

In the interior of the convent — cloister: permit from ecclesiastical authorities — is the famous fresco by P. Cavallini, Last Judgement (1293) where Byzantine elements are subjected to a Classical motif. The painter may thus be considered a forerunner of the new movement.

We turn down v. Anicia — right — and reach the church of S. Francesco a Ripa (17th cent.) where St. Francis lived. Artistically it is important for the statue of Blessed L. Albertoni (Bernini, 1674).

On Sunday mornings in v. Porta Portese — nearby — there is the Flea Market which has become quite a tourist attraction. Down v. S. Francesco a Ripa and beyond Vle Trastevere, we take the first left — v. Natale d. Grande — and reach Pza S. Cosimato and the architectural complex which bears its name.

We continue along v. Roma Libera and beyond v. Morosini and v. E. Dandolo passing Villa Sciarra (Wurts), now a public park. Proceeding to Vle Glorioso, we turn right, v. Fabrizi and at the end, v. Garibaldi — left — is the church of **San Pietro** in Montorio (B. Pontelli, 1481. Ring at N. 1), so-called because an erroneous tradition held it to be the spot where the Saint was martyred, and also for the golden colour of the soil. The church bears distinct Renaissance characteristics, and is important moreover for the works of two prominent artists: the Flagellation — first chapel to the right — by Sebastiano del Piombo, 1518, and the Coronation and Virtues, — vault, second chapel to the right — by B. Peruzzi. Interesting is the fact that Beatrice Cenci is buried under the steps of the main altar without an inscription.

Outstanding in the field of architecture for its clear Renaissance character is the Tempietto by Bramante (1502), in the courtyard to the right of the church. It is considered the starting point of Renaissance architecture.

We continue to the Fontana Paola (F. Ponzio, 1612) whose columns once decorated the Temple of Minerva in the Forum of Nerva. It is a water display similar to the Fountain of Moses. The main fountain cascades into a large basin under three arches, surmounted by a frontispiece, with emblems of the Borghese (Paul V). Entering from the right, we may visit the gardens at the rear. To the left — v. Garibaldi — we reach Porta S. Pancrazio (19th cent.) and continue to il Vascello, where in 1849 Garibaldi's men fought for the defence of Rome.

Farther ahead is Villa Belrespiro or Doria-Pamphili. It is a vast park arranged in gardens — Italian and English — with nymphaeums, and cultivated with pines and other trees. The Casino delle Allegrezze is the jewel of the entire complex. In this masterpiece by A. Algardi (1650) the staircases, the façade and the ornamentations show a great change in style from the days of the Farnesina.

Here also is the Casino dei Quattro Venti, another famous name during the defence of Rome. Beyond it rises the basilica of S. Pancrazio (5th cent.) with the catacombs of Octavilla.

We return to Porta S. Pancrazio and take a left turn to the **Janiculum Promenade.** On one side appears the façade of Michelangelo's house, transported from its original site on the Capitoline and here rebuilt. In the square — farther ahead — which affords a splendid panorama of Rome is the monument to Garibaldi (Gallori, 19th cent.). The hero is represented on horseback in a momentary pause glancing toward the Vatican. Busts of many of his men stand near him along the promenade amid the flower beds, and at a short distance, his wife Anita. Down the stairs beyond the Lighthouse we may view the trunk of Tasso's oak. The poet died in the nearby convent of S. Onofrio the day before his laureation on the Capitoline, 24/4/1595.

Roman Forum

Via Sacra

Arch of
Septimius Severus

Braccio Nuovo

S. Maria
in Aracoeli

Columns
of the temple
of the Dioscuri

Senatorio Palace

Palace of the
Conservatori

Piazza del
Campidoglio

53

IMP. CAESARI DIVI ANTONINI E DIVI HADRIANI
NEPOTI DIVI TRAIANI PARTHICI PRONEPOTI DIVI
NERVAE ABNEPOTI M. AVRELIO ANTONINO
AVG. GERM. SARM. PONT. MAX. TRIB. POT. XX
IMP. VI. COS. III. P.P. · S · P · Q · R

Capitol and Capitoline Museums — Palatine and Forums
Colosseum and Golden House — Arch of Constantine
Circus Maximus and Piazza della Bocca della Verità

This itinerary may be covered on foot in a day.

From the Capitol to the Forum, to the Palatine and the Caelium runs our visit to the ruins in the heart of ancient Rome; and the fragmented columns, the arches, the empty caverns, recall the life and customs, the crowds, the misery and splendour of the capital of the world 2000 years ago.

The buildings, then transformed for use by the new cult, indicate the urgent need the primitive church had to adapt Roman grandiosity to her present spiritual requirements; and she dramatically faced the majesty of ancient monuments, limiting the zone round about and letting nature and man take care of the rest.

The damaged arches, the theatres transformed into bastions, the truncated towers, give evidence to bitter Mediaeval feuds among the people, nobles and clergy abetted by powerful interests. The new buildings on the Capitoline Hill and their arrangement, facing away from the Forum, testify to the triumph of the papacy over the people of Rome and the world of antiquity.

CAPITOL

Nowadays, the Capitol may be reached from Piazza d'Aracoeli along a stairway, and by a road open to traffic; it is a trapezoidal square, with an equestrian statue of Marcus Aurelius in the centre, the Senatorial Palace at the far side, Palazzo dei Conservatori and the New Wing. This spatial arrangement is known as inverse perspective. It is embellished at the front by the marbles of the Dioscuri (found in 1583, Theatre of Pompeii), the Trophies of Marius and statues of Constantine and Constantius II. To the left of the stairway is the statue of Cola di Rienzo who was massacred here in 1354 while escaping in disguise; and, farther up, in an enclosure, the She-wolf, symbol of the city.

Michelangelo conceived this plan in the XVI cent. The attention of the visitor is focused on the structure at the far side — the horizontality of the other two leads the eye in that direction — with the portal centred on a façade flanked by staircases and surmounted by the Patarina, the tower of the commune; the statue of Marcus Aurelius is lifelike in the gesture of the hand, in the human, majestic visage.

Marcus Aurelius (161—180) was the emperor-philosopher, one of the most ferocious enemies of Christianity. He sought to destroy it through systematic persecutions because, deny-

The Capitol as seen from the Roman Forum (Plastic model of the town of Rome at the time of Constantine).

ing emperor-worship, it undermined the very foundations of the established order. He was, however, a man of action enlightened by a superior concept of justice. His statue was preserved because it was thought to be of Constantine.

The limited space is reflected in the architecture, now on a more human scale. Square and statue therefore blend to form the first modern urban complex. Michelangelo, in effect, forced by circumstance — the few visible ruins in the Forum were overgrown by orchards and vineyards while urban activies took place in the Campus Martius — developed the Capitol, signalling a new epoch in the orientation of the city.

The Capitoline Museum

(Sixtus IV, 1471; opened to the public since 1734)

Reclining in the narrow atrium is the River god, Marforio, one of the « talking » statues of Rome. The only means of criticizing the deeds of influential persons and ridiculing bizarre occurrences of everyday life was to secretly post lampoons on certain sculptures which in that manner became known as talking statues. To the right is the Egyptian collection of sculptures removed from the Temple of Isis in the Campus Martius; to the left, articles illustrating oriental cults; other sculptures may be found on the groundfloor to the right.

On the floor above a few works of great artistic value are displayed. We follow along the gallery, and in the first room to the right — of the doves — two mosaics may be noted on the walls: the doves drinking from a basin are achievements of a very refined sort — from the Villa of Hadrian — and, equally delicate, masks of the II cent. Farther ahead — right — we enter the Cabinet of Capitoline **Venus,** graced with soft, exquisite contours, a Roman copy in Parian marble of an original statue dating from the Hellenistic period. At the end of the gallery is a statue of Probus (33), one of the emperors of the decline (276—282) elected and put to death by soldiers who claimed he overworked them; though much to the dismay of many who considered him valiant and dutiful.

At the far side, we cross the Hall of the Emperors — 65 busts —, of the Philosophers — 75 busts — and reach the Great Hall. Here on pedestals, in the centre, are two admirable statues which illustrate the stimulus of love — Cupids — in youth — Laughing Centaur — and in old age — Weeping Centaur. The various elements which comprise them create elation in the one and desperation in the other, reflected with such immediacy of expression as to startle the observer.

Fascinating, against the far wall near the door, is the delicate sadness pervading the face of the Wounded Amazon (33): a replica of an original V cent. B. C. statue by Cresilas. Through the Hall of the Faun — note the outstanding Laughing Faun — we reach the Hall of the Gladiator.

In the centre is the **Dying Gaul** slowly sinking on one arm, his youthful body reflecting a vivid sense of pride and resignation before death. The torque around the neck and the hair style reveal a typical Gaul. This moving statue is a replica of a 3rd cent. B. C. bronze original.

Palazzo dei Conservatori

The museum originated with Sixtus IV in 1471. In the court-yard are the colossal remnants — head, hand — of the statue of Constantine, once in the basilica. Upstairs on the second landing we encounter the solitary statue of Charles of Anjou (Arnolfo di Cambio, 13th cent.). Like a Roman emperor the seated statue is surmounted with a regal head and distant gaze. This statue could be considered a symbol of the monarchy. King Charles, having defeated Manfred and Conradin (13th cent.), became sovereign of the Kingdom of the Two Sicilies and exerted much influence upon the papal states. With this statue, mediaeval sculpture emerged from the religious orbit and entered into the service of other masters.

Through the doorway to the right, we enter the Halls of the Conservatori, which were the formal rooms of the commune. The frescoes, tapestries, sculptures and carved doors that comprise this sumptuous setting, as well as the events that took place here and the persons who participated in them are very dear to the Roman people.

At the entrance are the gigantic statues of Urban VIII (Bernini, 1635—39) and Innocent X (Algardi, 1645) in similar, polemical poses.

Next we enter the Hall of the Captains and continue to the following room for a view of **Boy with a Thorn,** an admirable statue, noble in the simple gesture of the young boy extracting a thorn from his foot: a 1st cent. B. C. creation; and **Camillus** with delicate, youthful contours. In the following room is the bronze **She-Wolf,** symbol of the city, a core of strength ready to spring (6th-5th cent. B. C.). We cross the remaining rooms and reach the landing; next — right — is the Museum of Palazzo dei Conservatori. A few stairs to the right lead up to the Gallery of the Orti Lamiani where the Esquiline **Venus** stands, a young woman sculptured in the act of winding a band around her hair. We follow along the various rooms, interesting for their sculptures and inscriptions; then return to the gallery and cross the rooms on the opposite side.

At the far side we descend the staircase. Here are the remnants of the Temple of Capitoline Jupiter, built in 509 B. C., the gigantic blocks of which furnish some idea of early Roman costructions.

Other remnants of the temple may be seen in the New Wing (to the left). There is the interesting Apollo the Archer (5th cent. B. C.), a statue filled with tension, concentrated in the sharp, lean face. We return, and now proceed to the right entering the New Museum, where there are still more remains of the temple. The marble cube (9) is historically most interesting in that it was first the urn for the ashes of Agrippina and later, in Mediaeval times, a measure of grain for the population. Several sculptures are arranged in the garden.

We return to the statue of Charles and go up to the 3rd floor where the Capitoline **Picture Gallery** is laid out (Benedict

XIV, 1748). It contains works of the 16th—18th cent., outstanding among which are the following:

(Cini Collection, right) John the Baptist by Caravaggio. The painting dominates the far side of the narrow gallery, rich with porcelains, and its subject stands out in contrasts of light and shadow. His cold smile shows that the painter was still adhering to a pattern; but the free and independent composition and the chiaroscuro disclose true art. In the hall at the end (Fuga, 1748): the vigorous statue in gilded bronze of Hercules. This is a representation of superhuman strength created with simple means: a torso rising in levels, a small head in 3/4 position, the club sustained by the powerful wrist.

In the Room of Saint Petronella — exit to the right —, so called from the Guercino masterpiece which covers the far wall, is the Gypsy telling a fortune, by Caravaggio. The painting is based on a moment of incredulity and suspense, achieved by the blacks contrasting with the various light coloured garments and the background.

We return to the ticket office and request a visit to the Tabularium, the archives building of ancient Rome (1st cent. B. C.), famous for its portico, the oldest in existence.

From the square, to the left of Palazzo dei Conservatori, we go up beyond Vignola's portico to Palazzo Caffarelli, now the seat of the Communal Antiquarium, where Victory, the statue of the Curia, disputed on by Symmachus and St. Ambrose among others, may be seen.

Returning to the Capitoline Square, we go up the opposite staircase and enter, left, the basilica of **S. Maria in Aracoeli**. The interior with its 22 ancient columns — « a cubiculo Augustorum » is carved on the 3rd one to the left — and fine 16th cent. ceiling, conveys a sense of serene balance. Despite the 13th cent. façade rising high above the stairway (124 steps) built in 1348, this construction on the Arx goes back to the empire; and, though its origins are unknown, legend has it that the Sibyl here foretold to Augustus the coming of the Son of God.

Of religious interest are the remains of St. Helen contained in an urn-altar under the tabernacle in the left transept, and the Christ Child to whom thousands of children from all parts of the world write. From an artistic point of view: the frescoes of the Chapel of S. Bernardino — 1st right — (Pinturicchio, 1485). The events here narrated have a legendary air about them, the characters are sweetly perplexed, the landscapes luminous; the colours delicate: gradations of greys and yellows in refined 15th cent. taste.

We retrace our steps to the Capitoline Square and, to the right of the Senatorial Palace, go down to the **belvedere wall** for a delightful panorama of the Forum.

In this space, animated by a characteristic harmony, one can distinguish a few columns, two triumphal arches, brick constructions, churches roundabout, a campanile, some arcades of the Colosseum at the far side and, on the right, the dark caverns of the tree-covered Palatine.

It is an ispiring incomparable view. This was the heart of the Rome of Augustus, of Trajan, a city of one million inhabitants, the largest the world had ever known. The surroundings shone with marbles and gold, were ennobled by palaces, temples, markets. The Forum — from Foras = a place outside the walls — was a centre of activity, most intense around noontime. Everywhere, the noisy crowd was about its business. From the altars rose columns of smoke from sacrificial offerings, from the law courts thundered the voice of the advocate, from the rostrum a son pronounced an elegy on his dead father, while all along the **Via Sacra** the funeral proceeded. First came the flautist evoking sadness, then the professional mourners, the slaves followed next wearing wax masks of the ancestors; and then the deceased, laid on an open bier with the symbols of his rank, followed by his wife, tearing her hair in despair, and the closest relatives. Meanwhile, with words and jests the mime pirouetted along bantering the habits of the departed. Their curiosity aroused, the crowd momentarily made way for them.

Elsewhere, the throng envied the prosperous usurer reclining on the cushions of his litter on his way to the Arch of the Argentarii or it scoffed at a rich courtesan who from time to time drew back the curtains of her litter. Here, tradesmen round the basilica bawled the virtues of their wares displayed in the streets, and booksellers under the stalls of the Argiletum lured their clientele with a rare piece; while the veteran, full of years and wounds, dozed between the columns of the Temple of Vesta. It was a colourful crowd where unlimited luxury rubbed shoulders with the most dire misery. This world first underwent a decline, then the barbarians overran it in waves of destruction; the temples, unroofed, soon fell to pieces, earthquakes and floods destroyed and buried the columns and arches. Men in uncivilized fury stripped the monuments of their marbles and statues casting some into lime kilns, shattering others to bits for mosaics. And so the ruins were born.

We go down to v. di Mte Tarpeio — this name recalls the precipice whence traitors fell headlong to their deaths —, then, left — v. del Tempio di Giove —, continue along v. del Foro Romano. To the left is the portico of the Dii Consentes, remnants of the Temple of Vespasian and that of Concord — which commemorates the Concord reached between patricians and plebeians in 367 B. C.

Now we enter the Mamertine Prison where, below, in the Tullianum — a prison and death chamber during Roman times — Jugurtha and Vercingetorix among others were executed. On the right rises the church of Ss. Luca e Martina, built on the Secretarium Senatus. Here, Pietro da Cortona built his most elegant façade. To one side, on the left, is the **Forum of Caesar** with the columns of the Temple of Venus Genetrix, protectress of the Gens Iulia.

We cross v. dei Fori Imperiali, where on the left appear the truncated columns of the Basilica Ulpia in the Forum of Trajan — Apollodorus of Damascus —, dominated by the isolated, intact **Column of Trajan** (40 m.). The famous reliefs which decorate it represent the events of Trajan's Campaigns in Dacia (101—103; 107—108) and were made with sensitivity and a refined technique. The most important episodes of the preparatory phase, the campaign itself and the conclusion,

Vatican
St. Peter

Tabularium

Temple
of Vespasian

Arch of
Septimius Severus

Temple of Castor
and Pollux

Via Sacra

Arch of Titus

Arch of
Constantine

Via Trionfale

Castel
S. Angelo

Church of
S. Maria
Aracoeli

Forum of Caesar

Curia

Basilica
of Maxentius

Temple of Venus
and Rome

Colosseum

follow in uninterrupted sequence and give us a nearly complete documentation of the events. They are more difficult to follow now owing to the present road level, and also to their lack of colours, which in antiquity gave them such force.

The church to the left is called S. Maria di Loreto, while the one to the right is dedicated to the Name of Mary.

We follow to the right where against the side of the Quirinal rise the arcades of Trajan's Market. — Apollodorus of Damascus; also reached from v. IV Novembre. This was one of ancient Rome's most important complexes and an independent urban centre with shops stocked with the most varied products — from pepper to fish —, offices, halls for meetings and transactions and, above, a centre of operations from where could supervised the movement of the crowd, of merchandise and an instant impression of the general situation could be had. It was an impressive monumental centre.

High up, to one side appears the airy loggia of the 14th cent. House of the Knights of Rhodes with its graceful Gothic balcony. Ahead opens the **Forum of Augustus** with the ruins of the Temple of Mars Ultor constructed after the victory at Philippi. The walls flanking it, probably ruins of the apses of two basilicas, are curvilinear, and Bernini most probably took this design in consideration in his project for Piazza S. Pietro.

Next is the **Forum of Nerva** or Transitorium with a portion of the Argiletum, the street that connected the Forum to the Subura, and the columns with a statue depicting Minerva (Rabirius).

Beyond this, to the left, at the far side of the Forums, we reach Piazza del Grillo and enter the House of the Knights of Rhodes, built on remains of Roman houses; then from the loggia above we can enjoy a stimulating view of the Forum and the Market of Trajan.

We cross v. dei Fori Imperiali and enter the

ROMAN FORUM

Immediately beyond the entrance, to the right, are the extensive, 100 m. remains of the **Basilica Aemilia,** 179 B. C., which enclosed a marvellous central hall (94×24 m.) divided by colonnades.

The **Basilica** with its covered porticoes and meeting halls was used in Roman times as a market and court of justice. Large private buildings often had a great assembly room divided into naves by columns and with an elevated area, the apse, like a public basilica or its meeting hall in minature. The early Christians met in these places which, after the Constantinian Edict, became churches, known as basilicas. Nowadays, Basilica is a title given to churches which enjoy certain ecclesiastical privileges.

We climb the stairway of the **Curia** where the Roman Senate met from the times of Hostilius (680 B. C.) to the fall of the Empire.

The voting method of the Roman Senate was picturesque — they literally took sides — and it certainly stressed the individual's sense of responsibility. From the benches where they sat, the Senators moved to the right side if in favour, while those not in favour went to the left. The high sense of duty and dignity which animated the **Patres Conscripti** — so the Senators were called — was revealed on numerous occasions. It suffices to recall the episode of 388 B. C. when the hordes of Brennus, a heroic barbarian Gaul, conquered Rome, sacking it, massacring its inhabitants, setting it on fire.

A Gaul, having reached the portals of the Curia, forced his way in and halted in a moment of indecision and perplexity before that assembly of men, rigid as statues in their white togas. Stepping over to one of them he tugged at his beard. The reaction of the Roman was immediate and violent while the others remained motionless. And all were slaughtered in their places. It owes its preservation to Honorius I who consecrated it in 625. Many have been the changes in the interior: missing is the statue of Victory, symbol of the state and the Roman army, before which the Senators performed rites; gone is the emperor's throne which stood at the far side flanked by the benches of the consuls who directed the assembly; and missing are the bronze doors, still extant.

The Curia was one with the Comitium, the square in front where people participated in decisions during the Republican epoch. The seals S.P.Q.R. found in all parts of Rome beneath the escutcheon of the city, signifies Senatus Populusque Romanus = the Senate and people of Rome, and denotes the equality of these two groups in decisions of government. Next is the Tomb of Romulus recalling the legendary origins of the city and the mysterious death of its founder. At the end, the harmonious proportions (23×25 m.) of the **Arch of Septimius Severus** (203) class it as a noteworthy work while the areas in relief — the prisoners — reflect a taste different from the perfect art of Trajan's age. The inscriptions, though, are important from a historical point of view; and the missing name, that of Geta, murdered by Caracalla, his brother, in 211 points to the corruption of the emperors. The Rostra nearby served as a platform for orators, and the name is derived from the rams, or rostra, of enemy warships taken as trophies and fastened onto the platform. Cicero spoke to the crowds from this platform; and from the rostra hung at different times the heads of Antony, Sulla, Cicero.

Before is stretched a vast square. Nearby is the centre of the city — umbilicus urbis — and here also was the golden mile post whence originated all roads leading to the boundaries of the Empire, and on which were designated the various distances. On the front of the rostra is the Column of Phocas bringing us to the year 608, politically one of Rome's worst moments, when the pope, pressed by the corrupt government of Byzantium was forced to sanction terrible acts. To arrive at the emperorship Phocas had murdered his five sons. The column, filched from some ancient monument was raised to him for having presented Boniface IV with the Pantheon, which was subsequently transformed into a church and thus preserved.

On the right, beyond the Via Sacra, are the remains of the **Basilica Iulia,** which recalls two members of the Gens Iulia — Julius Caesar, who had it built, rich with marbles and columns, between 55 and 44 B. C., and Octavian, who founded the Empire and settled the crisis of the Republic. From an urban view-point, the construction on the western end of the Forum balanced the Basilica Aemilia. It was a court of justice. The Temple of Saturn, behind, was considered an important structure for it held the state monies; it was sacked, however, by Caesar during the civil war. In front of this monument began one of Rome's most popular festivals, the Saturnalia. Next to the Basilica Iulia rises an essential element of the Forum panorama, the three white columns of the Temple of Castor and Pollux (484 B. C.), recalling the legend of the Dioscuri. In the centre is the Temple of Julius Caesar built by Octavian (29 B. C.) on the site where Caesar's body was burned and where Antony delivered his famous funeral oration.

We turn right and enter the church of **S. Maria Antiqua.** It is an imperial construction adapted to Christian use and its setting is permeated with a special atmosphere. The frescoes are very interesting for the iconography and the colours that link them with Roman technique of the late Empire.

From here, by way of the Clivus Victoriae (see the guardian), we can reach the Palatine. Returning to the Forum, on the right, rises the Temple and House of the Vestals, the most revered virgins of ancient Rome — with the right to sit next to the emperor at the circus —, custodians of the sacred fire which should never be allowed to go out. Such a breach of duty or the loss of their virginity were punishable with burial alive. On the opposite side of the Forum may be seen the columns of the Temple of Antoninus and Faustina (141), now the church of S. Lorenzo in Miranda. Following, on the same side, is the Temple of Divus Romulus, son of Maxentius (309).

We continue along the Via Sacra and reach the Arch of Titus, raised to commemorate the victories over the Jews and the destruction of the temple of Jerusalem (70).

To the right, we go up the Clivus Palatinus.

PALATINE

The Palatine is the hill where Romulus and Remus are said to have begun the building of ancient Rome.

The importance of the site lies in its proximity to the river — water supply — and its defensibility. The shepherds came down the hillside to fight the Sabines, to trade and discuss in the Forum, to conquer other tribes. Now rise Quadrimontium Rome and the Servian walls. The hill was very important during the rule of the kings. During the Republic it was inhabited above all by orators, and covered with temples. Here Augustus was born, and here he built his home, establishing thereby the residence of the emperor, and words Palatium, Palatinus, Palazzo thus became synonymous with

Palatine. The Palatine Stadium

imperial palace, regal or noble dwelling. And so it remained even during the High Middle Ages; meanwhile fortresses were built. Probably the heaviest destruction came about in the 16th cent. with the creation of the Farnese Gardens. A present-day visit to the Palatine reveals charming scenery shaded by thick vegetation, long vistas over Rome and a wealth of interesting ruins.

We first encounter the 16th cent. Farnese structure, where a wide view of the Forum may be had from the loggia. Beneath the adjacent garden lies the yet unexcavated palace of Tiberius. On the outer limit of the garden the most ancient remains (9th—8th cent. B. C.) of the zone were discovered: huts, wells and the Scalae Caci. Now we reach the House of Livia, wife of Augustus, interesting for the frescoes in Pompeiian style. Beyond Nero's Crypto-porticus we go up to the centre of the hill occupied by the ruins of the Flavian Palace, built by Domitian (Rabirius).

The frescoes and the spaciousness furnish an idea of the sumptuousness of the dwelling, whose most interesting room was the triclinium. To the right, round about the Antiquarium stretched the Domus Augustana or imperial palace (Domitian) inhabited up to the times of the Byzantine governors. It is worth visiting the Antiquarium which preserves works excavated on the hill, among which is the famous graffito of the Crucifix. Also to be seen are the Palatine Stadium and, to the right, remains of the Baths of Septimius Severus and the belvedere-terrace which affords an admirable view of the **Circus Maximus,** now transformed into a park. Here the Rape of the Sabines took place. The site between the Aventine and the Palatine was an ideal spot for a circus and the area was surrounded with walls during the final epoch of the Republic; it appears that its tiers of seats held 300,000 spectators.

To the right, we pass in front of the Paedagogium and proceed along Vle Velabrum and the Clivus Victoriae where the Lupercal, the cave where Romulus and Remus were suckled by the She-wolf, may have been located. We return to the Forum and exit by the entrance door.

We now turn right and reach the church of **Ss. Cosmas and Damian** (Pope Felix, 527). On this spot once stood the library in the Forum of Peace. The apse is notable for its mosaics (6th cent.).

They represent Jesus with Ss. Peter and Paul, Cosmas and Damian, Theodore and Felix IV who is seen presenting a model of the church. These strong figures reveal the type of men who inhabited the world of Odoacer, Theodoric and Belisarius (5th—6th cent.). We retrace our steps and proceed to the right, along v. dei Fori, where a few geographical maps in marble, set into the walls, document the development of Rome up to the conquest of the world. Farther ahead we take the road to the right which leads to the Forum of Peace.

Now we go down to the Basilica of Maxentius and Constantine (306—312) built as a seat of justice. Only a few gigantic side bays decorated with lacunars remain, together with some blocks fallen from the ceiling scattered in the enclosure. These remains nevertheless suffice to convey an idea of the overpowering construction that probably inspired Bramante in his plans of St. Peter's. Some of the columns that once embellished it are now scattered about Rome.

From this side, to the right, we reach the church of **S. Francesca Romana** or S. Maria Nuova, built in the Forum of Peace, an ancient but much modernized building. There is a beautiful 17th cent. ceiling and also a striking 11th cent. mosaic in the apse representing the Madonna and Child between Ss. Peter and Andrew to the right, James and John to the left. From a religious point of view: the two stones — right transept — with the footprints of St. Peter who prayed here for the punishment of Simon Magus; the venerated image on the high altar (12th cent.); and, in the sacristy, a panel of the 5th cent. called S. Maria Nuova.

The Colosseum faces the exit and all around are the rows of columns of the Temple of Venus and Rome (Hadrian, 121—136) the largest and richest of the city. It was built in two cellas united by apses with statues of the two divinities. Apollodorus of Damascus criticized the statues for their gigantic proportions and paid for it with his life.

The roof was covered with gilded tiles which, in the 7th cent., went to cover ancient St. Peter's.

COLOSSEUM

We are now standing before the Flavian Amphitheatre or Colosseum (Vespasian and Titus, 72—80), so-called for the presence of a statue-colossus of Nero. It is the best known structure of ancient Rome and symbolizes the historical continuity of the city down the centuries. In the 7th cent. the Venerable Bede commented: « when the Colosseum falls, so shall Rome fall, and the world ». It was erected by Jewish prisoners and rises in three order of arcades — Doric, Ionic, Corinthian — surmounted by an order of pilasters.

This level is interesting for its squared blocks which are pierced where the corbels were inserted for the support of the velarium, or awning. It was used from the 100 day inauguration period (when 5000 wild beasts were killed) to the times of Honorius, following the sacrifice of Telemachus. From then on, after the martyrdom of numerous Christians, systematic attempts were made to destroy this construction. The arena — the name is derived from the sand used to cover up the blood — measured 75×46 m. With its stone — travertine, tufa and bricks of concrete — Pzo Venezia, Pzo della Cancelleria, the Port of Ripetta and St. Peter's were built. It was declared sacred by Benedict XIV (18th cent.) in commemoration of all the martyrs. The pillaging of this inexhaustible quarry was thus put to an end. It seated 50,000 people who entered and exited through 80 archways: the central ones toward the Caelium and opposite were for the authorities; another, toward the Forum of Peace for the gladiators — Sanavivaria —, while the opposite one

was for the corpses — Libitinaria —. The substructure was used as a warehouse and for cages which when opened admitted men and beasts to the sphere of action.

Outside the Colosseum remnants of Roman pavement may be seen; part of the base of the Colossus; and the Meta Sudans. Nearby is the

Arch of Constantine

It was erected by the senate in honour of Constantine in the year 315, and in the dedicatory inscription there is mention of the new God of the Christians. It dates from a period of low artistic achievement, and because the builders were conscious of this situation, they inserted panels and medallions from other monuments in the upper part.

We turn left, and at the top of the incline, between v. Labicana and v. S. Giovanni in Laterano, view the remains of Rome's largest gymnasium, the Ludus Magnus, where gladiators trained.

The term **Gladiator** is derived from gladius (short sword) and signifies one who wields it. The gladiator's games were of warlike origin and go back to the martial exercises of Roman youth in the Campus Martius. The privilege of belonging to the Roman army was then reserved to the Roman citizen (civis romanus). The gladiator, on the contrary, was, at least at first always a slave, a prisoner who could by fighting in the arena and surviving, redeem himself from his conditions. Later, in times of decadence, Roman citizens and emperors took part in the games at the circus.

Beyond v. Labicana, we turn right into Vle della Domus Aurea, to visit the remains of Nero's Golden House, the

Domus Aurea.

Thus named was the complex of constructions — 3000 rooms —, statues, avenues, artificial lakes, which stretched from the Oppius to the Velia, from the Palatine to the Caelium and whose dimensions led the Roman to exclaim, « We'd best look for living quarters in Veii, there's no more room here. » The mordant, critical spirit of the Romans has survived the centuries and seems inexhaustible.

It was built following the fire in 64; its significance for many was that thousands of Christians, impaled and covered with pitch, slowly illumined — human torches — the nights in the Neronian gardens; for others it is the beginning of the city's first organic construction: structures in regular blocks divided by avenues, limits in height for the houses — many apartment houses had collapsed on the tenants — vast spaces, porticoes. Nero, traditionally the most bloodthirsty emperor, in this way claims at least some merit.

The structure, of which only these ruins remain, covered 400×200 m. and was the first royal palace erected in Rome. As can be noted, it is a complex of rooms, corridors, peristyles, covered with «grotesque» vault decorations. This type of decoration may be seen above all in the Golden Hall, where Fabullus seems to have given the best of his art; and the pupils of Raphael here placed their signatures.

Obviously, a centre of such size in Rome's most crowded quarter could not escape being destroyed at its owner's death: the statues were removed, the buildings demolished to create new ones; and on this central building Apollodorus of Damascus, the architect in the service of Trajan, raised the Thermae which were spacious and functional and served as a model for all others. Remains of the Baths of Trajan may be seen on the Oppian Hill, at Villa Brancaccio.

Returning to the Arch of Constantine we proceed to the ancient **Via dei Trionfi,** now known as v. S. Gregorio, along which the triumphs proceeded toward the Via Sacra in the Forum and the Capitol where they concluded. Now, midway — right — is the main entrance to the Palatine, and farther ahead to the left, the church of S. Gregorio. Pope Gregory (6th cent.) displayed decisive action for the benefit of the church by disciplining her internal organization, raising the living standards of the population, facing foreign enemies — Lombards — with weapons of charity, and evangelizing England. We have now reached the area of the Circus Maximus from where the imposing ruins of the Septizonium (Palatine) may be seen.

We proceed, right, to the Piazza **della Bocca della Verità,** in antiquity known as the Forum Boarium.

It is one of the most fascinating places in Rome owing to the atmosphere created by the two temples — that of Fortuna Virilis, 100 B. C., in Greek-Italic style, and that of Vesta, circular, of the Augustan age — and the church of S. Maria in Cosmedin (decoration) of the 7th cent. with a 12th cent. campanile. The first two bestow a sense of nearly self-conscious greatness, reserve, and, considering their age, immortality. In the interior of the church, below road level, we enjoy the fascination of primitive simplicity. In this context, not even the baroque fountain seems to clash. The Arch of Janus stands in the background, its niches empty, and, beyond, against the church of S. Giorgio in Velabro, the Arch of the Argentarii from the period of Septimius Severus which recalls Caracalla who murdered his brother and removed from the monuments all traces of his memory. Here money-changers and jewellers met.

Moreover, near the slopes of the Palatine, rise the churches of S. Anastasia and S. Teodoro.

This zone between Palatine-Aventine and the river was very busy because of its convenient location and it comprised the port area where commodities for the city were unloaded. Ruins representing all the centuries may be seen here, from the mediaeval house of the Crescenzi, to the left going back up v. del Teatro di Marcello, to the church of S. Nicola in Carcere, which rises on the three temples of the Forum Olitorium (vegetable market), and above all the noble remains of the **Theatre of Marcellus** whose history of demolition, reconstruction and transformation can be traced back to the days of Caesar; it became very important — as a fortress — in the Middle Ages. It held 10,000 spectators in Roman times and consisted of a double order of arcades with an attic.

Finally, we go up the Capitoline slope to the belvedere wall and view the sunset over the Forums and the Palatine.

The temple of Venus and Rome, the Colossus (wherefrom the Colosseum derived its name), the Arch of Constantine (Plastic model of the town of Rome at the time of Constantine).

77

Piazza della Bocca della Verità. Church of S. Maria in Cosmedin

Via del Teatro di Marcello and Theatre of Marcellus

Palazzo Barberini,
Gallery.
Raphael Sanzio:
The Fornarina
(Portrait)

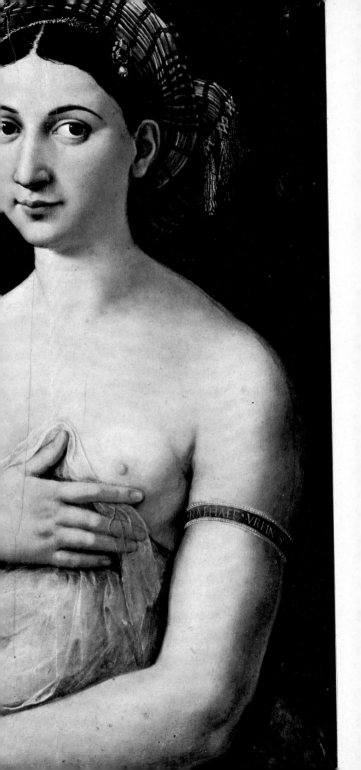

ITINERARY 3

Pantheon
Palaces: Venezia - Cancelleria - Farnese
Piazza Navona - Piazza di Spagna - Piazza del Popolo
Fountain of Trevi - Corso - Quirinale - Moses (S. Pietro in Vincoli)

This is a one day itinerary which is best covered partly on foot and partly by bus or car. For distances consult the map.

The visit to the **Campus Martius** and the **Subura** is conducted along the banks of the Tiber, in the low-lying area at the edge of the Forums and Esquiline, in places where the Romans of the Republic prepared themselves for war, and in the winding streets of ancient Rome's popular quarter. During the times of Augustus and Agrippa the Campus Martius was drained and porticoes, temples, baths rose along the v. Flaminia, as far as the mausoleum of Augustus; and the Subura continued in its picturesque way of life lighted now and then by the sinister flares of fires which firemen in the service of Augustus were unable to dominate.

In the darkest days of the High Middle Ages, the Campus Martius was white with marbles, puddly, dotted with campaniles and monasteries, while the few inhabitants lived like troglodytes in the caverns of the monuments. This area, though, acquired the importance of a centre when, in the 6th cent., all the inhabitants of the city flocked here, forced to abandon the hills when the aqueducts were cut off by Witigis, king of the Goths, and the river became the only source of drinking water. St. Peter's, moreover, became a centre respected by kings and people alike; and the Campus Martius was its direct dependency: here palaces and churches rose and streets were laid.

Complexes of the utmost interest may be found here, like the ancient Pantheon, or Piazza Navona, built on a site of antiquity, and expressions of a determined epoch like Piazza del Collegio Romano, di Spagna, del Popolo. And the Corso, that portion of the v. Flaminia up to the walls, so called because of its horse races, from the 16th cent. on became Rome's fashionable artery together with the adjacent streets, which at times follow ancient trails, like Alta Semita.

To this day, the greatness of the past may be noted in the superb palaces. And ancient poverty still lurks along the rundown staircases of houses coloured with clothes drying in the sun. Together, often contrasting stridently, they make this the most suitable itinerary to penetrate the character of the Roman people.

That complex of buildings — palace, church, palazzetto — and gardens which from the 15th cent. occupied part of the present Piazza Venezia and the site of the monument to Victor Emmanuel II, for one century served as the living quarters of popes and constituted the architectural centre of the transitional period from Mediaeval to Renaissance. **Palazzo Venezia** still maintains that feeling in the harmonious fusion of elements belonging to both periods — mediaeval fortress: tower, battlements, sturdiness; Renaissance taste: space, windows, portal —. The Basilica of S. Marco begun by Pope Marcus in the 4th cent. is, in its portico and elegant loggia, one of the jewels of the Early Renaissance (L. B. Alberti). The interior is interesting for the mosaic decorations of the apse (9th cent.) and the 15th cent. ceiling. The Palazzetto Venezia, also known as the S. Marco garden, where ambassadors and princes were received, is a rebuilt 15th cent. building.

On the exterior wall is a marble bust known as Madame Lucrezia, another of the city's « talking statues ».

We are now in the Pigna district; the name recalls the fountain once located in the garden.

The districts into which the mediaeval city was divided followed approximatively the districts of Augustus, and were designed for purposes of easing the maintenance of order and having a corps of militia ready for attack and defence: they were under the authority of a **Capo-Rione** or district head and in the Italian language it gradually came to signify knave, which thus sheds light on the character of the times. On one side of the square at the back of the Capitol and the Forums rises the monument to Victor Emmanuel II and the Unknown Soldier and, important for the history of the Risorgimento — Italy's national revival — the Museo Centrale del Risorgimento.

The Museum of Palazzo Venezia is arranged in the first floor Barbo and Cybo apartments and the Palazzetto and is interesting for the rare furniture of various epochs, for its paintings and the atmosphere of the rooms.

By way of v. del Plebiscito, to the right of the façade, and beyond v. degli Astalli, we reach **Piazza del Gesù**, from 1544 to 1556 residence (N. 45) of Ignatius di Loyola, Knight of Christ and founder of the Society of Jesus. Here rises Il Gesù, the mother church of the order, where he is buried.

The Jesuit Order arose with the Council of Trent which took an unwavering stand against Lutheran reforms and was inflexible with its own faithful, upholding, among other things, doctrine with dogma to make the contrast still more profound. The Order became interpreter of these theories and so, came to be a model of dogmatism and ecclesiastical discipline. Reactionary in the field of art, it established that every work of religious import should first be subjected to the judgement of a theologian.

In the atmosphere thus created — tribunals, critiques, accusations — the life of the Catholic lost all its charm and so it became necessary to transform the church into the most splendid centre of the community and to attract the individual with colour and grandiosity.
The church of the Gesù (begun 1568), prototype of Jesuit churches, reflects this spiritual moment in both façade and interior: the former (G. della Porta), with characteristic

elements doubled up — orders, niches — is a marvel of richness; the latter, with its vastness and sumptuousness seems bound to overwhelm the onlooker. All this is stressed in the interior, at two points: the vault fresco by Baciccia — Triumph of the Name of Jesus — and the chapel of St. Ignatius in the left transept (A. Pozzo, 1696—1700), the tomb of the Saint.

To fully appreciate this religious moment which so greatly influenced world government over the following centuries, and still does, particularly in what concerns the church, it is necessary to reach Piazza del Collegio Romano — across v. Plebiscito, v. d. Gesù, and to the right, v. Piè di Marmo — and, along v. S. Ignazio, Piazza S. Ignazio.

The brick construction of the **Collegio Romano** enclosed the principal preparatory institute for Jesuits whose method of education formed princes and kings and even to this day is at the base of a determined culture; it modelled a well-defined type of man and perfected a mode of behaviour.

It was the seat of the Victor Emmanuel National Library, the nucleus of which is formed by the Jesuit library of the Collegio Romano; housed here is the L. Pigorini Museum of Prehistory and Ethnography.

The church of St. Ignatius (1626—50) repeats the themes of the Gesù and in its complex of stuccoes, decorations and gold, it expresses a feeling of joyous festivity. Admirable in the urban arrangement of the square is the pleasing sceno-graphic taste of F. Raguzzini who accomplished it between 1727 and 1728.

We return by way of v. S. Ignazio and Piè di Marmo to Piazza Minerva.

Excavations in this zone have produced notable ruins of ancient monuments, for the most part of the Augustan period: in via dell'Arco della Ciambella and along v. di Torre Argentina, the Baths of Agrippa (27—25 B. C.) Rome's most ancient and luxurious, remains of which may also be seen behind the Pantheon; the Alexandrine Baths, against the church of S. Eustachio; and the Temple of Minerva, goddess of wisdom, after which the square is named.

PANTHEON

But the highlight is the Pantheon, antiquity's most important monument which, despite restorations, transformations and adaptations, is still the most perfect example of Roman build-ing methods. It was commissioned by Agrippa in 27 B. C. and dedicated to Mars and Venus, protectors of the Julian family. In fact, in the cella there was even a statue of the Divine Caesar. Under Titus (80), the building was severely damaged by fire and a complete reconstruction was ordered by Hadrian; hence, it is conceivable that the inscription above was transferred from the earlier building. The Rotunda, as the Pantheon is called, embraces the square before it, embel-lished by a fountain with an obelisk (Isis Campensis).

It is a structure whose feeling eludes us, as though beyond the organized simplicity of its plan and elevation it possesses other secrets. This dissatisfaction also derives from the fact that the edifice has survived intact, above a sea of ruins across two millennia and for a better understanding of it only feeble comparisons have been left us. It is formed by a cylinder — wall thickness, 6,20 m. —, a dome which covers it — 43,30×43,30 m. —, a deep porch — 33,10×13,50 m. — limiting the entrance with 16 monolithic columns and topped with bronze beams long since removed, with two niches at the far side, now empty. The bronze doors are original.

The originality and beauty of the monument arise from the contrast between the definite geometrical figure of the façade and the elusive rotundness of the rest. Also noteworthy is the fact that the present street level does not allow a full appreciation of the actual proportions. However, just inside it unfolds in its immensity, enveloping the onlooker from all sides: in this creation of volume, lies the organic quality of the building.

The sole source of light is from the central opening which measures 9 m. in diameter. Seven niches are carved into the lower part and decorated with columns and pilasters; the chapel at the end is topped by a wide arch which balances the one at the entrance. Above are the trabeation and the attic, in times past adorned with marbles, and above it rests the vault decorated with coffers which diminish in size toward the opening. At the end to the right, are two rooms of the Roman epoch, now used as a sacristy and chapel. All around are tombs and altars. In the second chapel is the tomb of Victor Emmanuel II, Italy's first king. The tomb of Raphael may be seen between the 5th and 6th chapels with the Madonna del Sasso, by Lorenzetto (1520) commissioned by Raphael, and the epitaph of Maria di Bibbiena, his betrothed. Following is the chapel-tomb of the second king of Italy and the tomb of Queen Margherita. Baldassarre Peruzzi is entombed in the next altar.

In the vicinity of the Pantheon, almost in recognition of its importance, are the following churches: S. Chiara, S. Eustachio, built on the house of the Saint, the Maddalena with its celebrated 18th sacristy, and S. Maria in Aquiro.

Flanking it is that remarkable monumental complex, **Piazza and church of S. Maria sopra Minerva:** the former is characterized by the elephant supporting the obelisk of Minerva (Temple of Isis Campensis, 4th cent. B. C.); the latter has a 17th cent. façade but its interior is Rome's only example of Gothic architecture.

Its atmosphere is altogether unique, and may be attributed in part to the memory of those buried here. Under the high altar St. Catherine of Siena (1348—80), that great personage who offered mystical love to popes and criminals; in the first apsidal chapel to the left, B. Angelico, painter of a serene faith; Leo X and Clement VII, the Medicean popes, in the wall behind the high altar, one facing the other: the former brought the papacy to its golden age and to the reformation; the latter, with the Sack of Rome, saw the end of an era. Interesting from an artistic viewpoint are Filippino Lippi's frescoes

(1489) in the Carafa chapel at the end of the right transept; the Risen Christ, a sculpture by Michelangelo (1521) on the exterior wall of the left presbytery.

Along v. S. Eusebio and d. Staderari we reach C.so del Rinascimento, which flanks the **Stadium of Domitian** on this side as does v. d. Anima on the other. Its arena corresponds to Piazza Navona, and the tiers of seats to the buildings round about. The Corso del Rinascimento, opened in 1938, boasts two notable buildings, Palazzo Madama now seat of the Senate, built by the Medici family in the 16th cent.: here lived the wife of Alexander: Madama Margherita. Leo X and Clement VII while they were cardinals; and Palazzo della Sapienza, built by Giacomo della Porta. The Roman University was located here in the days of Eugenius IV (1431—47).

In the interior may be seen the original church of S. Ivo alla Sapienza designed by Borromini together with the controversial spiral lantern that rests atop the cupola (1642—60). Another important edifice may be reached to the left of the Senate, and along v. S. Salvatore, **S. Luigi dei Francesi,** the church of the French. Migrations, wars, pilgrimages during the centuries of the High Middle Age led persons of different nations to Rome and, be it to assure the salvation of the soul, be it because of the high profits to be made, the most enterprising opened shops and small businesses in the Trastevere area round the old basilica of St. Peter. They provided lodgings for the newly arrived, gradually forming veritable colonies organized and sustained by the nations of origin. The growth of these colonies, protected by prelates, led to the erection of national churches, a clear manifestation of the universality of the Church.

S. Luigi dei Francesi was built in the 16th cent. Three paintings accomplished by Caravaggio in 1597 may be found in the 5th chapel of the left aisle: the Calling of St. Matthew; the Martyrdom of St. Matthew; St. Matthew and the Angel. The light forming the figures, the dull colours, the original, antimanneristic composition, are basic elements of these paintings. At the exit we turn left and, in v. d. Scrofa, take the first left, where the church of S. Agostino rises (Giacomo da Pietrasanta, 1479—83); its interior was remodelled in the 18th cent. At the third pilaster is the image of the prophet Isaiah (Raphael, 1512). At the end of the square to the right, we reach Piazza delle 5 Lune and again right all the way to v. Tor Sanguigna where in v. dell'Anima the church of the same name may be found. This is the Austrian church. Ahead to the right, in vicolo della Pace, rises S. Maria della Pace, built by B. Pontelli in 1480. In the interior are Raphael's admirable Sibyls, painted in 1514, and, next to the altar, one may enter the Cloister, Bramante's first Roman work, executed between 1500 and 1504.

We return by way of v. dei Lorenesi alongside the church of S. Nicola, and arrive at **Piazza Navona.**

With the Council of Trent the Catholic church cut off that part of herself which Luther had turned against her, and with the aid of the Society of Jesus she consolidated her internal affairs by means of organization and doctrine. One century after the Lutheran movement, the Church regained her confidence and again treated her own faithful tolerantly, granting maximum liberty within the limits of the Church. Augmented by nepotism and rivalry, the constant thought of the Popes in this period was to make of Rome the shining capital of Christianity, enriching her with churches, palaces, fountains, giving them a baroque aspect, probably the most pronounced of all her many faces.

Piazza Navona is the artistically splendid result of the rivalry between two artists — Bernini, Borromini — and a reflection of the enmity among powerful Roman families. Here, the spirit of Innocent X, buried in S. Agnese, may be felt; he would not hear of Bernini, the best artist of the times; yet, confronted with the originality of his designs, he permitted the construction of the fountain of the Four Rivers (1651) — Nile, Ganges, Danube, La Plata —. And the dispute with Borromini, builder (1653—57) of the church of S. Agnese in Agone, whose statue with hand to breast «insures» that the cupola shall not collapse, explodes in the frightened pose of the Ganges, and the covered head of Nile. The Obelisk, rising from a hollow in the rocks, where a thirsty lion bends his head to the water, demonstrates boldness of concept. And the threads with which Bernini one night «secured» it to make certain it should not fall, give further evidence to the not always pleasant contentions of the times.

Behind the curtains of Palazzo Pamphili looms the shadow of Olimpia Maidalchini, whom the people termed « Olim Pia », once pious.

Piazza Navona exactly repeats the dimensions of the stadium (240×65 m.) and even follows the curved form, though nowadays it can no longer be flooded as in the XVII cent. when rich carriages splashed through it. Contributing to the joyous atmosphere of the square is the rush of water, pouring in torrents from two other fountains — that of the Moor (designed by Bernini), and that of Neptune (Della Porta) —; and the square is permeated with unforgettable personality. Nowadays a popular festival takes place here on Epiphany.

At the end of the square, against Palazzo Braschi, is Pasquino, the city's most popular « talking statue ». Now, we take v. di San Pantaleo and in the square bearing the same name enter the Museo di Roma, interesting above all for its life-size figures representing scenes from Roman life of the last century, arranged on the groundfloor; and for the papal train. Through frescoes, sketches and paintings on the first floor, it is possible to view the transformations of the city and the habits and customs of the people. On the III and IV floors, paintings by Roman artists from the 19th cent. to the present day are arranged.

We cross Corso Vittorio Emanuele whose bridge links Piazza Venezia to the Vatican, and enter the Barracco Museum, worth visiting for its remains of ancient sculptures, many of which are originals, and many artistically noteworthy. We exit to the right and reach Piazza della Cancelleria where the **Palazzo della Cancelleria** stands; it is one of the most characteristic structures of the Renaissance period, built by A. Bregno and Bramante (1483—1517). Noteworthy on the façade are the Riario rose (Cardinal Raffaele) and the emblem

of the Della Rovere family. The building is faced with polished travertine and divided into three floors. Also admirable is the harmonious courtyard where 44 ancient columns removed from the church of S. Damaso may be found. The present church of S. Lorenzo in Damaso, built by Bramante, is part of the palace; it was restored in the last century, thus only the plan of the original is conserved — probably it was impaired in its grandiosity by the wealth of marbles.

We go to the front of the building, v. dei Baullari and, turning right for Campo dei Fiori, we can see, at the end, Palazzo Farnese.

The building we are now observing is the most striking example of a general urban movement in Rome: the palace rises at the centre of a plebeian quarter. Powerful families found it necessary to dominate a district in order to enlist soldiers and thereby derive power and prestige. The palace so situated expresses authority, strength and richness, arouses respect and fear, offers protection. The numerous palaces which embellished Rome throughout the Renaissance are built on this basic premise. The baroque or neoclassic palace, though located in a plebeian quarter, stresses, on the contrary, a spiritual poverty hidden by external luxury and grandiosity, or by the coldness of a false reaction. Another element of the Roman palace is constituted by the shops which can be noted on the secondary sides of the building: an element which reflects the economic situation of the city and recalls a very ancient tradition.

Campo dei Fiori, completely occupied by awnings and stands is the market-place of a popular zone. Dominating all that hubbub is the statue of Giordano Bruno, burnt alive here, on the spot where executions took place, in the year 1600. The environment is picturesque and vital. To the left of the square, Palazzo Pio stands on the ruins of Pompey's Theatre. We continue ahead: before us rises the superb **Palazzo Farnese.** The refinement of its floors, dominated by the famous cornice (Michelangelo) brings to a climax the Renaissance palace. The grandiose façade, the remarkable dimensions, the rhythmical spaces enhanced by columns and cornices, express confidence and solidity. Collaborators in its construction, which lasted over half a century and caused Pasquino to quip « a coin ... for the building! », were A. da Sangallo the Younger, Michelangelo and G. Della Porta. Also notable are the portico, courtyard and the gallery, frescoed by A. Carracci (1597—1604) as well as the grand hall. It is now the seat of the French Embassy and the interior may be visited on Sundays from 11—12.

Now, to the left of the palace, we take v. Capo di Ferro where stands Palazzo Spada with its 17th cent. Gallery; in Piazza dei Pellegrini to the left we follow along through v. Arco d. Monte, to the right Piazza d. Monte di Pietà and v. degli Specchi to Piazza B. Cairoli. We cross v. Arenula, centre of the Regola district, and continue along v. S. Maria d. Pianto. Between v. del Progresso and the Theatre of Marcellus is a characteristic zone inhabited by Jews, the Ghetto; it is enriched by ruins of once famous architecture like the

Porticus of Octavia (Augustus, 23 B. C.) that at one time contained a wealth of artistic works; by the church of S. Angelo in Pescheria, whence Cola di Rienzo left for the conquest of the Capitol; coloured with small mediaeval houses and Renaissance dwellings. It comprises a complex of hovels whose life creates a picturesque environment. It is dominated by the grey cupola of the Synagogue, built in 1904 in oriental style, probably the most obvious manifestation of recent freedom.

The Jews were in Rome in the first century of the Republic, and became more numerous with the growing attraction of the world capital. They lived in Trastevere where suspects and villains were relegated. Already in the first years of the Empire, they numbered 10,000 and Claudius wanted them deported, forcing them to disappear in order to survive. At the moment of Jerusalem's conquest and together with the spoils, borne triumphantly to Rome and deposited in the Temple of Saturn, 70,000 Jewish prisoners were led here as slaves — a condition shared by all prisoners of war — destined for forced labour. Other emperors opposed them for different motives: the desire to appropriate their riches, the need to reduce their importance — Simon Magus was one of them —, mixing them with the Christians — Jewish catacombs exist —; Caracalla, on the other hand, granted them Roman citizenship and all its rights.

Their social standing during the Fall and at the time of the Barbarians was equal to that of the Roman people. The Jews, rich and poor, were at times used and at times opposed; literature, however, always chose them to personify the most abject characteristics of human passions. During the Middle Ages they enjoyed no freedom: the quarter was surrounded by iron bars and they were forced to observe the curfew from sunset to dawn: at night the entrances were closed; they wore emblems of recognition (16th cent.): yellow cap and orange net; every year they bowed their heads at the senator's feet, who thus confirmed his dominion over the Jewish community; moreover, they were taxed 1130 florins, to cover the cost of the festivals in Agone and Testaccio. The Jews now live in all parts of the city as well as the ghetto.

We cross the narrow lanes of this zone where the contrasts of splendour and sordidness lend colour to the area, return to v. Pettinari, and at the level of Ponte Sisto, take v. Giulia, opened by Julius II, a fashionable street during the 16th cent.; and continue all the way to the end.

Here, round the church of S. Giovanni dei Fiorentini, was the centre of Rome's wealth and progress in the days of Alexander VI, Julius II, Leo X. We cross Cso Vittorio and by way of Arco della Fontanella, reach v. Banco di S. Spirito. Now we turn left and beyond Palazzo Cicciaporci, along vicolo del Curato enter v. di Panico and, first left and then right, v. dei Coronari. We are now at the centre of the two most important districts of 16th cent. Rome, **Ponte** and **Parione,** and these very streets witnessed the deeds and misdeeds of the times.

Here lived Raphael — left side of Palazzo Gabrielli —; in v. Mte Giordano is the Orsini fortress mentioned by Dante;

in v. Banchi Nuovi lived Aretino and Cellini and Agostino Chigi rose to fortune.

It is the zone where Michelangelo roamed, heartbroken, a victim of the times and of creative fire.

We reach the Napoleonic Museum, facing Ponte Umberto and, leaving behind Tor di Nona, site of the gallows, turn right into v. d. Orso. Here is the Hostaria dell'Orso, the hotel where, among others, Dante, the Florentine ambassador to Boniface VIII, Rabelais, Montaigne and Goethe stopped. We proceed to v. dei Portoghesi, v. d. Stelletta, and arrive in Campo Marzio, and along v. Uffici del Vicario to Piazza Montecitorio — it appears that the Roman centuries voted here — with its Obelisk of 594—89 B. C. and Palazzo Montecitorio (Bernini, 1650), seat of Parliament. Now we walk to **Piazza Colonna,** where the column of Marcus Aurelius may be found, distinguished by its carvings which illustrate events in the Germanic (171—73) and Sarmatic (174—75) wars. Galleria Colonna is one of the centres of modern Rome.

We take v. del Corso to the right: the palaces which flank it and its narrowness give it a heavy, severe aspect: 17th cent. To the right is Palazzo Doria-Pamphili and its Gallery arranged with paintings of the 16th to 18th cent. Among the most outstanding are: Ist wing — Rest during the Flight into Egypt, one of Caravaggio's early works; and — Room II, of the Cabinet — the famous portrait of Innocent X painted by Velasquez in 1650, one of his most beautiful works.

We retrace our steps and follow along the Corso, beyond Galleria Colonna. Farther ahead on the opposite side of v. d. Vite, is Palazzo Fiano, where ruins of the Ara Pacis Augustae were found, and which are now laid out in P. Augusto Imperatore, farther ahead, just before reaching the church of S. Carlo al Corso, along vicolo del Grottino.

In the square rises the rebuilt Mausoleum of Augustus. The **Ara Pacis** is a sculptured monument dedicated to the peace that Augustus wished to usher in with his reign and which after wars in Spain and Gaul seemed assured. This complex of marbles, sculptured with sensibility and refined technique, enclosed the sacrificial altar; and the carvings represent the processions and sacrifices of Augustus and the members of the imperial family. The characters are portrayed from life and are identifiable: Augustus, Livia, Agrippa, etc. It is an important accomplishment in that it denotes a new taste in Roman art. It dates from 13 to 9 B. C.

On the exterior wall is a bronze reproduction of the inscription recording the public life and deeds of Augustus, known as the Monumentum Ancyranum, from Ankara, the place where it was discovered.

We return to the Corso and proceed to **Piazza del Popolo**, a masterpiece by G. Valadier, 1816—20. For a full impression of the scenographic and artistically complete arrangement on all sides, we walk to the centre and up the few steps of the Fountain. This neo-classic accomplishment pivots upon the Flaminian Obelisk (1232—1200 B. C.) which rises on a pedestal decorated with four lions spouting water

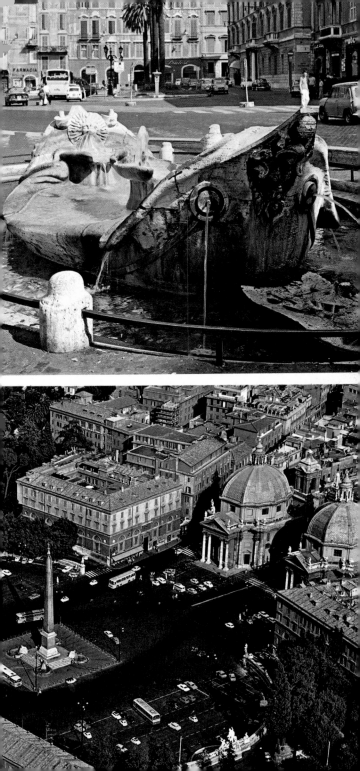

from their mouths. The space is enclosed between two semi-circles embellished with statues — the Seasons — and ennobled on one side by the churches of S. Maria in Montesanto and S. Maria dei Miracoli, and closed on the other by Porta del Popolo. From the slopes of the Pincian hill, arranged with statues on every tier, water pours in torrents and spouts from the square's numerous fountains filling it with freshness.

Besides the carvings of Porta del Popolo, by Bernini, another important monument on this side is the church of S. Maria del Popolo, a distinctive structure built by B. Pontelli and A. Bregno (1472—77). The interior is baroque in style.

This church, which is said to stand on the tomb of the Domitians where Nero was buried, was famous in Renaissance times, and some of the most powerful families of the period — Della Rovere, Cybo, Mellini, Chigi — had chapels and tombs here.

Most notable is the Chigi chapel, the second to the left, where the tomb of Agostino recalls the rich and famous banker, the illustrious patron of the Farnesina: and here too Raphael followed him, accomplishing the cartoons for the mosaics. The Duke of Candia and Vannozza are entombed in the right apsidal chapel. The fusion of art with richness is shown here in masterpieces of two centuries: from the frescoes of Pinturicchio, 1485—89, in the first chapel to the right, to the sculptures of Andrea Sansovino behind the high altar; to the conversion of St. Paul and Crucifixion of St. Peter, two painting by Caravaggio, realistic and immediate in their black and white contrasts.

A renowned centre even nowadays is **Piazza di Spagna** with its **Spanish Steps.** This is the heart of Settecento (18th cent.) romantic Rome, whose Café Greco rendezvous, at the beginning of v. Condotti, was frequented by such artists as Gogol and Stendhal, Liszt and Leopardi and d'Annunzio. John Keats died in the red house at the foot of the steps, 1821. It is a spectacular sight — the travertine steps with landings and balconies were built by F. de Sanctis, 1723—26 — characterized by the tall Sallustian Obelisk and the twin belfries of the church (16th cent.), and now by the flower stands.

The square below is really two triangles: Pza Mignanelli, south of which is Bernini's Propaganda Fide structure, with Pzo di Spagna to one side, and Pza di Spagna with the Barcaccia Fountain (P. Bernini, 1627—29), recalling the boat transported here by a Tiber flood. And the square stretches on in the greenery of its palms. On the neighbouring streets — Babuino, Margutta — antiquarians have shops, and artists, studios; while movie stars choose to be photographed on the fashionable Steps, a renowned meeting place.

Above, facing the church of Trinità dei Monti, we take v. Sistina, to the right, a street of 19th cent. Rome and reach Piazza Barberini, where the celebrated Fontana del Tritone (1632—37), a gift of Bernini to his patron, passes nearly unnoticed owing to the heavy traffic. The square is halfway between modern **Via Veneto,** known for its hotels, cafés, night spots and worldly life, and Piazza Colonna. The district crossed by Via Veneto was built in the Humbertan period, at the beginning of the century, on the site of Villa Ludovisi, remnants of which are a few trees in front of Palazzo Margherita, seat of the American Embassy, the enclosed parts around the Casino dell'Aurora, so called from its fresco by Guercino, and a few other green areas.

We continue — right — v. Quattro Fontane and midway, on the left, enter Palazzo Barberini (1625—33) whose architecture signals the onset of Baroque style, even though the structure recalls, in exaggerated manner, the motifs of the Farnesina. A few art collections have been set out here and comprise the **National Gallery of Ancient Art,** with works dating from the 13th to 18th cent. Among the paintings shown in the various rooms is the notable portrait painting by Raphael of his mistress, the Fornarina, in the chapel, and the renowned portrait of Henry the VIII by H. Holbein the Younger (1540).

Also outstanding is the fresco in the grand hall, the Triumph of Divine Providence, a masterpiece by Pietro da Cortona (1633—39).

Outside, we walk to the Quattro Fontane. From here we can see the obelisks of the Esquiline, the Quirinal and the Trinità. We turn right and reach the church of S. Carlino, thus known for its miniature dimensions — exactly those of one of St. Peter's pilasters —. Borromini worked at it more or less frequently from 1634—67, and left it unfinished. An organic complex, it reflects a typical moment of the Baroque era with its original architectural solutions. Farther ahead rises the elegant construction of S. Andrea al Quirinale, a Bernini masterpiece (1658—71) created in seeming contrast with S. Carlino. Now we reach Piazza del Quirinale, also known as Mte Cavallo, from its group of Dioscuri flanking the Obelisk.

Palazzo del Quirinale, built over a period of two centuries, was the papal residence from 1592 to 1870; now the President of the Republic lives here. The Courtyard is by D. Fontana. In the interior is the Pauline Chapel (XVII cent.) with the same dimensions as the Sistine. Outside to the left is the Palazzo della Consulta, the Cotitutional Court, and before it the low buildings of the papal stables.

We walk down by way of v. Dataria and v. S. Vincenzo to the **Fountain of Trevi.** One of the world's most popular, the small square lives by water that cascades into the great basin at the rate of 80,000 cubic metres daily. This « virgin water » recalls Agrippa who in 19 B. C., in order to set his Baths going ordered that water be conducted from a spring that a maiden had indicated to thirsty Roman soldiers. The name derives from this episode. The present imposing structure is by Nicolò Salvi, who from 1732—51 succeeded in accomplishing a noble work. The space 20×26 m., is decorated with columns, while below the arch appears Ocean drawn by sea horses among the rocks and water, falling in a thousand rivulets.

The visitor's interest pays homage to probably the most essential element of the city, water, and with the casting of a coin « to return to Rome » he pays a tribute of love and understanding to its spirit.

We return by way of v. S. Vincenzo and turn right in Piazza della Pilotta: here stand the buildings of one of Rome's most powerful families, the Colonnas. They rose to the papacy with Martin V (1417—31). The original basilica of Ss. Apostoli goes back to the 6th cent. and for centuries was a theatre for famous celebrations and festivals. Besides its works of art, the Colonna Gallery (v. della Pilotta, 17) is interesting for the rooms in which they are displayed, and for the rare relics owned by the family.

From Piazza Ss. Apostoli, we exit into v. C. Battisti, walk up v. IV Novembre and across Piazza Magnanapoli, whose name derives from an ancient bath, turn right into v. Panisperna, a winding street, and cross the Suburra of antiquity, where huts were crowded, and the streets filled with life.

At v. dei Serpenti, we turn right, and after crossing v. Cavour proceed to v. d. Annibaldi thereby reaching the church of **S. Pietro in Vincoli,** so called from the chains of St. Peter. The place is most interesting owing to the presence of Michelangelo's **Moses,** one of the few statues completed for the tomb of Julius II (1514—16). The statue is seated, with the head turned to one side looking toward the Jews gone astray, with a biblical beard falling in long curls, and a gigantic body, a symbol of divine justice.

Now we walk down toward the Colosseum and the Forums while the sunset animates this incomparable scene.

Borghese Gallery.
Raphael Sanzio:
Portrait of a Lady

ITINERARY 4

The Walls - Galleria Borghese - Baths of Diocletian and National Museum - S. Lorenzo
St. John Lateran - S. Maria Maggiore - S. Clemente
Appian way - St. Paul's outside the walls - Catacombs

The places described in this itinerary may be visited in a day by car, taxi or bus.

From Porta del Popolo to Porta S. Paolo we cover a considerable area and at the four main churches there is an ever present point of reference, the Walls, and another, equally important, the Catacombs: inherent in both are the causes which lead to the ruin of the Roman Empire.

The **Walls,** built by Aurelian between 270—275 are the most eloquent acknowledgement of the weakness of the Roman army, now unable to defend the city from the Barbarians who soon arrived at the destruction of the mythical inviolability of Rome; from the **Catacombs,** where Christian proselytizing over 250 years had spread like an oil stain, the principle of equality corroded the social, economic and religious apparatus of the Roman world.

Whether crossing the zone where there were once the gardens of the Pinci, Maecenas, and Sallust, rich with statues and nymphaeums, or penetrating the superb architectural ruins of the Baths of Diocletian or Caracalla, one encountered crowds of people dedicated to idleness and pleasure. The slaves and the people of the Suburra, went beyond the walls and frequented the catacombs.

Over these caverns, where relics are conserved of those who saw Christ, and of others by the thousands who testified with their lives to the new Truth, rose the great basilicas as soon as Constantine conceded it: St. Paul's outside the Walls, S. Sebastiano, S. Lorenzo. And on the ruins of pagan edifices, toward the heart of Rome, St. John Lateran, and S. Maria Maggiore. We shall cover stretches of famous highways: the Salaria, Nomentana, Prenestina, Casilina and, above all, the most beautiful avenue in the world, the Appian Way, where tombs and remains of aqueducts create that element of tradition and fascination of the Roman countryside.

The exterior part of Porta del Popolo was designed by Michelangelo. We proceed along v. Flaminia, leaving behind on our right, the entrance to Villa Borghese. We can now view the Tempietto di S. Andrea (Vignola, 1554), the Flaminio Stadium (Nervi, 1959) and the Olympic Sports Palace (Nervi, 1954). Above, to the right, is the luxurious Parioli Quarter. The modern city districts — deluxe, popular, middle-class — comprise buildings of nearly equal aspect and function in an effort to cope with the growing necessities of life and the lack of time; ancient contrasts of palace and popular dwelling are thus diminished. We return to the level of Pte del Risorgimento, take v. delle Belle Arti and reach the Villa of Julius III (Vignola, 1551—53), where one of the world's most important Etruscan Museums, the **National Museum of Villa Giulia,** is located.

Among the artistic accomplishment of the Etruscans, still shrouded in mystery, are the outstanding serenity of expression, the human concept of death, and the delicacy and continuity of affection after death. Among the masterpieces are: (Room IV) the struggle between Apollo and Hercules; (Room VIII) the Sarcophagus with sculptures of a husband and wife reclining; (Room 33) the Ficoroni casket that bears one of the first examples of the Latin language.

At the exit is the National Gallery of Modern Art. Housed here are works of Italy's most renowned artists of various schools, from the early 18th cent. to the present day.

Returning, we reach the curve — at the end — and, first to the right and then left, enter Vle dell'Uccelliera which leads to the

BORGHESE GALLERY

The numerous halls on the ground floor — Museum — where sculptures are displayed, and on the first floor — Gallery — where the paintings may be found, are decorated with 18th cent. frescoes.

Notable in the vast entrance hall are the mosaics of the Roman period — hunting scenes and combats —. To the right is the Hall of Pauline Borghese, sister of Napoleon: its name derives from the marble statue in the centre, carved by Canova (1805). The female figure, reclining on a couch, rests on her right hand, the head posed in the manner of a Venus Victrix — hair, band, eyes, fingers — while the minute, transparent body seems to quiver. This renowned work is considered a masterpiece.

The next rooms is focused on one of Bernini's early works, the statue of David, rich in movement and impetus, two elements that characterize the Baroque style. These constituents are expressed with more immediacy in the following room, where **Apollo** has barely touched **Daphne,** who is transformed into a plant as she flees. The group — Bernini, 1624 — is an expression of that moment in which touch and transformation take place.

In touching the beauty, the breathless motion of the god's pursuit suffers no pause but continues on through leaves and branches and roots just sprouted but already so vigorous that they firmly encircle the body, whose skin toughens into bark. The marble seems moulded like wax and is suited to receive and express a subtle sensitivity.

In the great hall — here, at the right hand corner, we walk up to the gallery — Bernini is again present with the Rape of Proserpine and, in the last room, the statue of Truth. The Gallery contains some of the world's most renowed paintings. To the right (IX) the Entombment 369, and Portrait of a Lady 371, by Raphael. The religious painting reflects, in figures and colour, the mysticism and delicacy of Umbria which move the spirit to piety; and the portrait shows that lightness of touch — hair, eyes, clothing — that constitutes the spiritual essence of the subject. Roundabout are: Madonna and Child, St. John and Angels, 348, by Botticelli wherein line creates the typical hair and faces dominated by bewildered, abstract looks; and, 401, Madonna and Child by Perugino.

In Room X, besides Andrea del Sarto's manneristic Madonna and Child (1514), there are, 326, Venus and Eros depicted as thin, pinkish figures in the German manner, by L. Cranach, and (444) the Baptist, by A. Bronzino.

We cross Rooms XI, XII, XIII for a general view, and reach Hall XIV. Six of Caravaggio's paintings are displayed here: 267, the Baptist in the desert; 56, St. Jerome; 136, Boy with a fruit basket; 534, Bacchus; 455, David with the head of Goliath; 110 Madonna dei Palafrenieri.

The artist's style here is in decided contrast with his former traditional 16th cent. works and the images are evoked from shadows by means of powerful light. In some cases the figures are still enveloped in the atmosphere of the times but for the most part they are completely detached and actual in the reality of the setting, in the poses and expressions. Realism is the most important factor in Caravaggio's art, and the harshness and drama of his own life are reflected in his paintings, and the protagonists are expressions of his particular social level: gamesters, assassins, harlots. Because of this, the clergy of St. Peter's, in 1605, refused that masterpiece which is the Madonna dei Palafrenieri.

In the hall may be seen a portrait of Cardinal Scipione Borghese, founder of the gallery.

In Room XV, following, the Descent from the Cross by P. P. Rubens (Rome, 1605). The painter expressed with colour and atmosphere the official feelings of the times, so different from the art and life of Caravaggio.

We cross rooms XVI, XVII, XVIII and arrive at the last two. In Room XIX is one of Correggio's masterpieces, Danaë. The arrangement of the painting expresses a complete moral decadence and, in the perfectly assimilated influences of the various schools, the end of an epoch. Equally famous is the Circe by Dossi.

Room XX displays two celebrated works: **Sacred and Profane Love by Titian** (1512), and a panel by Antonello da Messina, Portrait of a Man (1473). In the former, two young women are seated in different poses on the edge of a sarcophagus where a cupid is plucking the petals from a rose. The landscapes behind each are different: to the right, framing the luxurious, fleshy body, is a village by the sea with a campanile which stands out against the sunset; to the left, for the young woman in rich array, a castle in the Veneto hills amid sweet treelined countryside. Both women are lost in their own thoughts, which no one seems able to penetrate. For us, it is enough to enjoy the painting in its sensitive colours which express a mature, nearly courtlike art.

In the second painting, the face of the gentleman is lifelike in the forceful penetration of the eyes and the determination of the lips. Antonello, who was then in Venice, brought from Flanders not only the secrets of new oilpainting but also the realism of the Flemish school, which forms the essence of the portrait. Also in this room are two paintings attributed to Giorgione.

At the exit we cross the avenues of the park, with its temples, monuments, artificial lakes, and bridle path; a **panorama** of the city can be had from the **Pincian Hill.**

Here stretched the gardens of the ancient Pinci.

From the main entrance to the park, facing Porta del Popolo, we go up the road to the left skirting the Muro Torto. This was one of the weakest parts of the walls, as is all this stretch to Porta Pia, where in 410 Alaric burst into Rome, the first Barbarian to conquer the capital of the world.

At Porta Pinciana we are in direct communication with v. Veneto. We proceed along Corso D'Italia to Pza Fiume, where the v. Salaria begins: the name derives from the salt commerce the Romans carried on with the Sabines. And we continue through Porta Pia, which closes v. XX Settembre — the ancient Alta Semita — which is named after that day in 1870 when the Italian soldiers entered the city and made it capital of the new Italian Kingdom.

On the opposite side of Porta Pia begins the v. Nomentana, from Nomentum, the modern Mentana. Outside the gate — v. Villini, 52 — are the Catacombs of S. Nicomede. The **Catacombs,** which in Greek signifies, «by the hollow» are subterranean galleries in storeys — total length 900 Km. and 3 to 25 metres in depth, for the most part still stopped up.

Their wall inscriptions, the primitive altars surrounded by a wider space, the remains of corpses, indicate them as places for burial — as was the custom practised in Rome —, for reunions, for prayer. Their fresco decorations, moreover, are the most vivid testimony of early Christianity, when symbolism in order to be understood was grafted onto Roman painting and sculpture brightening them with a new spiritual life. The statue of Hermes became the Good Shepherd.

The v. Nomentana skirts Villa Torlonia in whose park stretch 9 Km. of Jewish catacombs (2nd—3rd cent.). We continue to the basilica of S. Agnese, which despite restorations, is still one of the best examples of Proto-Christian construction. The interior is embellished with ancient columns and a mosaic (7th cent.) illustrating St. Agnes between Popes Symmachus and Honorius. At the entrance to the narthex, one may proceed for a visit to the Catacombs. **S. Costanza,** nearby, is a mausoleum (4th cent.) built for Constance and Helen, daughters of Constantine. The interior — circular plan, double columns, ambulatory — is Roman in style and claims the most ancient Christian mosaics yet brought to light (4th cent.).

In via Asmara 6, are the Catacombs of the Cimitero Maggiore. To the left, we reach v. Salaria, at the level of Piazza Priscilla; ring at n. 430 for a visit to the Catacombs of Priscilla, located in the park of Villa Ada, where frescoes illustrate various symbolic representations of the primitive religion.

We return to Porta Pia and then, by way of v. XX Settembre — here stretched the luxurious gardens of Sallust — follow all the way to Piazza S. Bernardo, where the church of S. Maria della Vittoria rises. Also located here are the church of S. Susanna (the official American church), built on the spot of the Saint's martyrdom, and the Fountain of Acqua Felice (16th cent.), commissioned by Pope Sixtus V.

We turn left and reach Piazza Esedra, now della Repubblica, with its sensational **Fountain of the Naiads.** The square corresponds to the gymnasium area of the ancient baths, and the edifices roundabout to seats for the spectators. The rooms of the Baths including the tepidarium were converted into the Church of S. Maria degli Angeli and transformed by Michelangelo. Both the square and the church offer a spectacular view of building methods and spatial domination, so natural to the ancient Romans. The church is the burial place of S. Rosa, C. Maratta, P. Tenerani; and is artistically important for the St. Sebastian by Domenichino.

The Baths of Diocletian (3rd—4th cent.) whose main entrance was located where the Great Cloister is, on the opposite side of the square, comprised a central building surrounded by nymphaeums, gymnasiums and gardens. It covered an area of 376×371 metres, and 3.000 persons could bathe there. These establishments were favoured by Romans of every level as places to pass an afternoon with friends, being massaged and oiled by slaves and bathing, and later to watch competitions or read or simply to enjoy the shady gardens.

So refined were the pleasures of conversation and society that the Romans brought to utter architectural perfection the building of the Forica — of which many remains still exist —, enhanced with statues and stuccoes and animated with fountains. A great part of Roman life was spent in the baths and at table. In the interior is the

MUSEO NAZIONALE ROMANO or delle Terme

The rooms are formed by the remaining walls, and the walls themselves, in brick and solid as rock, are impressive for their proportions and size. And the decapitated, mutilated statues, arranged in ancient niches furnish some idea of the purely decorative function that the Roman conceived for sculpture. This function was also applied to painting: a painting was never hung on a wall for it would have destroyed its continuity; they were set in. Architecture then, is the art which distinguishes the Roman from all other peoples of antiquity, and the perfection to which he brought the Arch and the Vault, adapting them to the most varied needs of daily life — bridges, aqueducts — are representations of a self-assured, organizing, ambitious type of man. At the entrance we walk directly to Room II where reconstructions of parts of Hadrian's Temple repeat the feeling of grandeur. Room IV (follow the numbers) is interesting for the brightness of the mosaic illustrating a Nilotic landscape.

Room VII is distinguished for its original pavement. In Room X the sepulchre of G. S. Platorino has been reconstructed. Now we reach the garden, a mere fraction of the original, and enter the museum, divided into various sections. The Ludovisi collection, arranged in the small Cloister — left, beyond the entrance — is renowned for a few valuable sculptures, among which are the Gaul stabbing himself with his wife, and the Ludovisi Throne. The former is a replica of a bronze dating from around the middle of the 3rd cent. B. C., dedicated to King Attalus I, conqueror of the Gauls. It illustrates a dying young woman and her husband who while sustaining her with one hand, with the other plunges the sword into his body in an act of pride and desperation. The beauty and attraction of the group consists in the successful expression of these sentiments.

The Throne (8570) comprises original marble sculptures of the 5th cent. B. C. and is so called for its shape. In the centre is the Birth of Venus, a female figure being lifted from the waters by two nymphs and, at the sides, symbols of Sacred and Profane Love, a clothed female and a nude one.

The values of these sculptures are the sensibility of the expressions, the delicacy of the lines and a vague feeling of sadness which captivates and holds the observer. In the same section two other original sculptures may be enjoyed: (8598) Head of a goddess, 5th cent. B. C. and the fearful Erinys (8650), the hair clinging together with sweat. Among the sculptures of the cloister, the dreamy Ares Ludovisi is very well known.

The New Halls — doorway facing the entrance — house very famous sculptures. Beyond the Apollo del Tevere in Room 2, we enter the Hall of the Masterpieces (3). Immediately recognizable is the **Discobolus** (56039) of Castelporziano, from the place where it was found: a young man with muscles tensed and just on the verge of hurling the disk. It is a faithful replica of Myron's original bronze. The Niobid of the Sallustian gardens (72274) is a nude copy of a 4th cent. B.C. statue whose expression is captured in that moment in which the fatal arrow is being wrested from the wound. Fascinating is the feeling of humanity in the gesture. The **Venus** of Cyrene (72115) depicts a woman emerged from the waters.

This is probably the most naturalistic representation of the goddess. The Ephebus of Subiaco — from Nero's villa — recalls the myth of Niobe's daughters and the concept of death. In the face of it, in fact, all efforts fail. The statue illustrates this moment with great efficacy. The observer is struck by the empty eye sockets of the Boxer at rest (1055), sadly anticipating his tragic destiny.

The Maiden of Anzio after 2000 years was uncovered by a sea breaker at Anzio beach and is attractive for its simple youthful grace. The statue (56230) in Room 6 of Augustus of v. Labicana, after the place where it was found, depicts the emperor, with head covered, fulfilling his function as pontifex maximus, or chief priest of the Roman state, the visage set in an expression of majestic gravity. From these examples one can conclude that man and the important manifestations of his existence — birth, struggles, religious functions, death — constitute the basis of ancient art; and while in the Greek world the figure lives in serene idealization, the **Portrait,** modelled from a death mask, of Roman statuary, brings man back into the orbit of the crudest reality. These rooms and the garden — the great Cloister was arranged according to a design by Michelangelo — house a great collection of sculptures and mosaics, for the most part restored.

On the first floor, on the other hand, some rooms are decorated with original frescoes and stuccoes, removed from their places of origin — Villa Livia at Prima Porta, Farnesina — in order to conserve them more conveniently.

We walk down to Piazza dei Cinquecento — commemorating the 500 who died at Dogali in 1887 — where before us stands the functional Termini Railway Station. Roundabout are notable ruins of the Servian walls. We then turn left into v. Vicenza crossing a modern quarter, and continue to Castro Pretorio, the camp of the praetorians built in 23 by Sejanus, minister of Tiberius. The **Praetorians** were the emperor's special corps, and as the quality of imperial rule declined they gradually acquired such authority as to place on the throne the highest paying aspirant. The place then became the property of the Jesuits, who called it Macao, and later a barracks. Now it houses the Vittorio Emanuele II, National Library.

We continue, right, along v. Tiburtina (from Tibur, Tivoli) to Ple Tiburtino, the basilica of S. Lorenzo and the Verano, the city's cemetery. The building of the **Basilica of S. Lorenzo** was restored in 1949; as a church it ranks among the most important of the city for its tradition and relics. At first it was formed by two buildings connected by apses: one commissioned by Constantine (330) and the other by Sixtus III, a century later. The apses were demolished in the 8th cent. giving way to a large hall. The Portico is by Vassalletto (13th cent.) and the campanile belongs to the 12th cent. The most interesting elements of the interior are the ancient columns, the ambos and the paschal candelabrum, the Ciborium and the 12th cent. Cloister. In the crypt under the high altar are relics of Ss. Lawrence, Stephen and Justin, as well as the Chapel of Pius IX at the far side of the underlying basilica of Constantine.

We return, right to Vle del Verano and re-enter through **Porta Maggiore** (Claudius, 52) built to support the conduits of Aqua Claudia. Here originate v. Prenestina and v. Casilina, also known as Labicana. The exterior part of the gate is characterized by the dark holes of the sepulchre of Eurysaces, a baker, proud of the trade that had made him rich. The Basilica of Porta Maggiore, N. 7, to the left, is a building which dates from the 1st cent. and is interesting for its architecture and stucco decorations; it was used by a mystical sect.

We re-enter the city. In front, along v. Statilia, run the arcades of the Neronian aqueduct. Then we turn left, v. Eleniana, and enter the church of S. Croce in Gerusalemme, or Basilica Sessoriana. It seems Constantine (320) had it adapted as a church within the building of Palazzo Sesso-

Porta S. Paolo. Pyramid of Caius Cestius

riano, residence of the emperors during the late Empire, in order to preserve relics of the soil of Calvary, now in the Chapel of St. Helena (end, right). The church is also interesting for the relics of the Cross, located in the Cappella delle Reliquie, which Helena, Constantine's mother, brought back from Jerusalem. The present building is in 18th cent. taste. At the exit we turn for v. C. Felice and reach Porta di S. Giovanni (16th cent.). Beyond it opens v. Appia Nuova, which crosses the S. Giovanni Quarter, one of the city's most densely populated areas. The most authentic expression of this population may be witnessed on the feastday of St. John, the patron saint, when the streets and the area about the basilica resound with joyous tumult and torchlight processions illumine the night.

Piazza S. Giovanni was not designed as a piazza but is a vast space bordered by famous structures: the basilica and palace of St. John Lateran, the niche-apse of the dining room of the Patriarchium, the Obelisk (37 m., 1400 B. C.) and the Baptistery. The residence of the popes from the time of Constantine until they moved to Avignon (1305) was the Patriarchium. This name signifies a whole complex of buildings and gardens, of the Byzantine type, defended by walls; they were destroyed by fire and pillage during the High Middle Ages. The popes, in fact, on return from Avignon favoured the Vatican over all other city palaces as their residence.

The present basilica of **St. John Lateran,** named after the ancient Roman family who owned dwellings and land in this area, is a baroque building (Borromini, 17th cent.) with elements from previous structures. The façade is a masterpiece by A. Galilei, who also built the portico where a statue of Constantine may be found. The interior is an expression of greatness and wealth, with its vastness (130 m.), gildings (ceiling, 16th cent.), statues and plastic decorations (17th cent.). Among the many interesting works worth remembering are: the Tabernacle (14th cent.) at the centre of the transept which protects the altar where only the pope may say Mass.

It encloses a wooden altar where it seems the first popes said Mass. The mosaic of the apse is by J. Torriti and Jacopo da Camerino; the fresco attributed to Giotto — first pilaster to the right — depicts Boniface VIII proclaiming the Jubilee of 1300. From a religious point of view, it is moving to remember the great events which took place here: the coronations and humiliations, the population on certain days could plunder at will, soldiers sacked and set fire to buildings. The tomb of Cardinal Ranuccio Farnese — last pilaster to the right — recalls the typical figure of an epoch. Historically, the tomb of Riccardo degli Annibaldi — at the start of the left aisle — evokes the power of mediaeval families, and the civil wars that brought Rome to the edge of total destruction (14th cent: 15,000 inhabitants); the tomb of one of the greatest popes, Innocent III (1198—1216) is against the wall of the first right apsidal chapel.

All these, though, are mere allusions to typical figures of different epochs; but in order to fully appreciate its place in the history of the world, it is well to bear in mind that each pope, upon election, here took possession of his church with its rites, feasts, traditional processions.

The **Cloister** — entrance, end of left aisle — is an inspiring space (13th cent.) bounded by columns of the most varied shapes, some of which are decorated with very effective mosaics (Vassalletto). The portico now houses sculptures, tombstones, inscriptions. The Baptistery, built upon a nymphaeum of Roman times, is restored. Octagonal in shape, it served as a model for other buildings of its kind. The columns support an architrave upon which rests another order of columns.

Round this space chapels were built at different times: the Baptist, in the 5th cent., where the original bronze doors are kept; S. Secunda, S. Venanzio and S. Giovanni Evangelista. The Lateran Palace is a monotonous construction of the 16th cent. (D. Fontana). It now houses on its various floors, the Pagan, Christian and Missionary Ethnological Museums with interesting sculptural remains originating from different parts of the city and territory. Among the valuable works worthy of mention in the Pagan Museum are the beautiful mosaics from the Baths of Caracalla in Rooms IV and V; and for their descriptive value, the reliefs decorating the sepulchre of the Haterii of Centumcelle in Room VIII. The diverse elements — sarcophagi, inscriptions — that comprise the Christian and Epigraphical Museums were removed from Catacombs and ancient basilicas and are an aid to a better understanding of the first period of Christianity.

The **Scala Santa,** built in the 16th cent. (D. Fontana) is named after the central steps which the faithful climb on their knees. They were transferred here from the Patriarchium, and are said to be the ones Christ ascended on his way to meet Pilate. The steps — 28, in marble — now lead to the Chapel of S. Lorenzo, called the Sancta Sanctorum owing to the great number of relics preserved here. This is a 13th cent. chapel with cosmatesque decorations, an image of the Redeemer, painted by some divine hand and usually covered, and three marble portals originating from the Praetorium of Jerusalem.

Following the visit we go to the right hand side of the square and enter via Merulana, formerly the site of the houses and gardens of the Meruli, an old Roman family; we continue to the end where there is the

Basilica of S. Maria Maggiore

It is one of the four patriarchal basilicas of Rome, together with St. Peter's, St. John Lateran and St. Paul's outside the Walls. The building is renowned for its tradition, its present aspect and its decorative elements. The original construction goes back to the 5th cent., and would link itself with the basilica of Pope Liberius — it is also known as the Liberiana — who planned the building on the spot where, one night in August, snow fell. Nowadays the building has two façades: one with a portico, where a statue of Philip IV of Spain, the

Pyramid of Caius Caestius (Plastic model of the town of Rome at the time of Constantine).

Catholic king, is set and a Loggia decorated with mosaics (Rusuti, 13th cent.) is a masterpiece by F. Fuga, 18th cent.; the other one, on Piazza dell'Esquilino is rich with marbles and statues of the baroque period (F. Ponzio, C. Rainaldi, D. Fontana).

The three-aisled Interior (86 m.), has a balanced aspect — 40 columns — and is baroque in taste. Of utmost interest, for an undestanding of the art of the late Empire, are the mosaic panels that form a continuous band on the central architrave (5th cent.), those on the triumphal arch (5th cent.), and the 13th cent. apsidal mosaic by J. Torriti. The Sistine Chapel built for Sixtus V — hence the name — in the 17th cent. by D. Fontana, and the Pauline Chapel, opposite, are both typical baroque works.

To appreciate Byzantine art in Rome we should visit the nearby church of **S. Prassede** — v. di S. Prassede — in whose S. Zeno Chapel (Paschal I, 9th cent.) is a delicate cycle of mosaics, a beautiful pavement decoration and an original architectural structure. Still more mosaics cover the triumphal arch and the apse. To the right of the nave, midway, is the site of the well where S. Prassede collected the blood and bones of martyrs. The church of S. Pudenziana — v. Urbana — built on the house where Peter is believed to have been the guest of Pudens, offers a 4th cent. apsidal mosaic and others of the 11th cent. situated in the Marian oratory.

We return by way of v. Merulana; about halfway we turn right at v. Mecenate and, at the end, right, v. Labicana. Turn left, v. S. Giovanni, known as the «Main Road» because the ponti-fical cortege passes here on coronation day. Midway to the left rises the Basilica of **S. Clemente.**

The upper part of the construction dates from the 12th cent. and still possesses that style in some parts, though suffo-cated by 18th cent. restoration, while the lower part is of the 4th cent. Typical elements of the primitive church are displayed in the interior: a raised choir, ambo, candelabrum for the paschal candle and the characteristic ciborium protect-ing the relics of St. Clement. The apsidal area, moreover, is dominated by an inspiring triumph of the Cross, a 12th cent. mosaic. Frescoes by Masolino da Panicale (1430) adorn the chapel of S. Caterina — at the beginning of the left aisle.

The lower church is interesting for its space, now interrupted by supporting piers, and its frescoes (11th—12th cent.) nar-rating episodes from the lives of Ss. Clement and Alexius; and Sisinius.

We return to the main road and, midway, turn right for v. dei Querceti and then left for v. dei Ss. Quattro where the church of the Ss. Quattro Coronati may be enjoyed in a setting of mediaeval constructions. At the end of the street, we turn right v. di S. Stefano Rotondo, where a church by the same name rises. It belongs to the 5th cent. and conserves the style of Roman constructions and the ancient columns. We reach the end and turn right at v. della Navicella, then left, v. S. Paolo della Croce. Now we proceed halfway where there is the church of Ss. Giovanni e Paolo (5th cent.) whose aspect, above all in the interior, is mainly 18th cent.

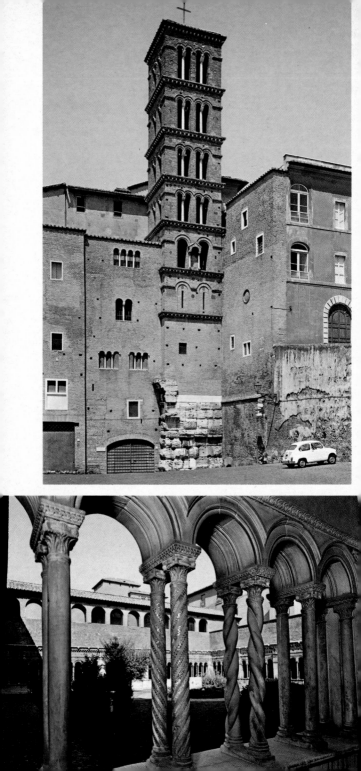

In the substructure many ancient ruins may be seen. We continue, right, to Clivo di Scauro. A the end to the left, is the church of S. Gregorio Magno, built on the property of the great pope. Proceeding left to via delle Camene, and across v. delle Terme we go up to the **Baths of Caracalla.** It was the most perfect bathing establishment in Rome up to the 6th cent.; and was prized for the richness and beauty of its marbles, statues and decorations. Now only imposing ruins remain.

We turn right, cross Ple Numa Pompilio, and along the street to the left — Porta Capena — reach the Porta Latina (Belisarius). Just outside, we take the right hand Viale delle Mura Latine and continue through Porta S. Sebastiano (6th cent.) and on to the

APPIAN WAY

Opened by Appius Claudius Caecus in 312 B. C., this first Roman road ran all the way to Capua; paved with basalt rock and flanked by footpaths, it reached all the way to Brindisi thus becoming a direct means of communication with the Orient. The first stretch, just outside the walls, was embellished on either side with tombs, mausoleums, statues, tumuli, as though the dead were still taking part in terrestrial events and participating in the parades of troops off to the wars or returning victorious with their triumphs, or in the corteges of kings and queens — Cleopatra — paying homage to Rome. Or as though mutely accepting the respects paid them by friends and relatives. It was the most beautiful road in the world and, all along it, the living and the dead were comrades. The tumuli and mausoleums became fortresses and prisons; the dead were dispersed leaving space for the living. Transformations continued through the centuries: the statues were removed, decapitated; the tombs crumbled.

Now the district is inhabited by millionaires; and the Appian way is asphalted.

Recognizable at the start is the church of «Quo Vadis», marking the spot where Christ appeared to Peter, who then returned to Rome and martyrdom. The Catacombs of St. Calixtus (N. 110) follow — only 20 Km. of them have been explored — and N. 119, the Jewish catacombs.

Next are the Basilica of St. Sebastian (4th cent.) reconstructed in the 18th cent., and the catacombs. Ahead are the Catacombs of S. Domitilla, a Christian who belonged to the Flavian family. Next, to the left, in the shape of mediaeval tower, is the unique tomb of Cecilia Metella. Continuing along under pines and cypresses, we see statues, tumuli, urns and in the countryside, remnants of aqueducts which lend a touch of solemnity and romance to the landscape. A trip to the Appian Way leaves one a bit sad and regretful.

We return left, by way of v. delle Sette Chiese and reach the **Basilica of St. Paul's outside the Walls.**

The present building belongs to the 19th cent., while the ancient one of the 4th cent. was destroyed by fire in 1823.

The Portico is 19th cent. The interior with its 80 columns and grandiose space is in Roman basilican style. Noteworthy are the Ciborium by Arnolfo di Cambio (1285), the apsidal Mosaics, the 262 mosaic Portraits of popes, the Candelabrum for the paschal candle (12th cent.) and the beautiful Cloister by Vassalletto (1210).

We continue on to Piazza di Porta S. Paolo (4th cent.) where the Pyramid of Caius Cestius (22×27 m.), with its sepulchral chamber (12 B. C.) may be found. Through the gate, we take, left, the street leading to the Protestant Cemetery, where Shelley and Keats lie. We are now at the Testaccio, a hill formed by broken amphoras, famous for its games and popular festivals. Returning to the gate we go left, v. Marmorata, where marbles were dumped in Roman times, many of which have been brought to light. We turn right into Lung. Aventino and again right, Clivo di R. Savella.

Up on the Aventine are the churches of S. Sabina, renowned for its doors, S. Alessio, and farther ahead toward the centre, S. Prisca. Walking down toward Piazzale Romolo e Remo we can enjoy the sunset over the Circus Maximus and the Palatine.

Ostia Antica - Tivoli - Cervèteri - Bracciano
Palestrina - Frascati - Castel Gandolfo

A visit to Rome's environs may be made by car, bus or train. A considerable amount of time is necessary due to the distances involved and heavy traffic.

Ostia Antica (Km. 23)

The excavation zone may be reached by way of the Autostrada del Mare. We take a right turn at about 6 Km. from Lido di Ostia.

The visit is interesting for the vast, serene Roman countryside characterized by pine woods and by the excavations that reveal the building system of a Roman town.

A straight road, Decumanus Maximus, originates at Porta Romana, the excavation entrance. It is flanked by various buildings (Insulae) divided in blocks by means of streets intersecting at right angles. On both sides, along its length run shorter parallel streets that alleviate the heavy traffic and link districts of secondary importance.

The buildings which may now be identified are the Baths facing Piazzale della Vittoria; farther ahead, the Baths of Neptune opposite via di Sabazeo. Following on the same side are the Theatre with the Temple of Ceres at the rear, and the House of Apuleius nearby. The Caserma dei Vigili (Firemen's barracks) is well worth a visit. Outstanding is the Guildhouse where mosaics of various trades may be seen.

These excavations have brought to light precious archaeological material now housed in the Museum, in a building to the right, beyond the car park. Not far from the Museum is the Casa dei Dipinti (House of Paintings), an interesting example of condominium housing, similar to our present day blocks of flats. We turn left at the corner of the Museum and following along the porticoed street known as Cardo Maximus, whose North-South course traverses the centre of the city. The Forum is located here, ennobled by the Temple of the Capitoline Triad — Capitolium —, a building found in all Roman cities, and opposite, the Temple of Rome and Augustus.

The ruins and the very plan of the city, which at its zenith had a population of 100.000, give us some idea of the importance of Ostia as the capital's merchandise-distributing centre. Ostia, like Rome, suffered destruction and ruin, aided, moreover, by the silting up of the harbour, the fury of invaders — Ostia was Rome's front against Barbarians advancing by sea — and the slow decline of the surrounding countryside, an easy prey to marshes and malaria.

Beyond the Temple of Rome and Augustus, the Cardo Maximus stretches all the way to the Necropolis and Porta Laurentina.

We return to the Forum where, facing the Basilica, is the Curia. Then we proceed along the Decumanus which terminates at Porta Marina.

The area we are now crossing has a wealth of monuments among which, beyond the gate along via degli Horrea Epagathiana, are the beautiful House of Cupid and Psyche, rich with columns and marbles, and the temple of Mithras on via della Foce.

Tivoli (Km. 31)

We proceed along via Tiburtina which just outside of town is flanked by large buildings. Towards the countryside the road narrows and becomes hilly. Modern industrial complexes alternate with huts. As the view now widens on both sides villages clinging to hilltops may be seen to the left. Past the few villages stretching along the roadsides, a steep hill rises before us. We shall soon distinguish modern buildings, here incongruous and nearly paradoxical. We turn right at the foot of the slope and proceed to the

Villa of Hadrian (Hadrian 125—134)

This ancient zone felt the influence of Rome. In those days it was thickly wooded and, as may be witnessed from the ruins, had a wealth of temples and tombs: the Romans sought it as place of serenity and pleasure. Hadrian's Villa, that was to have evoked in him the noblest architecture and the greatest luxury he had seen on his endless travels, is the best example.

The Emperor did not enjoy it for long, however, for he died only a few years after its completion; his successors, taken by the measure of its plan and the beauty of nature, added artistic works to it.

At the fall of the Empire, the villa underwent sacking and destruction; what was left still fills the museums of Rome and the world. They are statues, mosaics, highly refined columns, testifying to an ideal aristocratic beauty.

Beyond the car park and bar, the first structure one comes upon is known as the **Poecile.** This was decorated with paintings and recalled the Portico of Athens. Here too, promenades took place under porticoes built on to the sides of the wall. The building, however, differed in form and size (232×97 metres). On the opposite side, accessible from the outside, were the Cento Camerelle, small rooms for the praetorians. Though the exact names of the various places can no longer be ascertained, considering the times, we are probably not far from reality in supposing that this body guard protected the Emperor even in his pleasure haunt. At the far side, towards the right, a valley called **Canopus** was excavated, and not only did it recall to the Emperor the luxurious Egyptian city frequented by a rich Alexandrian society, but also Antinous, a favourite, drowned mysteriously in the waters of the Nile.

The imposing project (195×75 m.) following a natural depression of the land, was deepened at the bottom and reinforced with walls at the sides.

We retrace our steps toward what is probably the most astounding complex, the **Natatorium.** This circular structure was built for the purpose of surrounding with water (Euripus) an island reached by means of revolving bridges. On the island stood an edifice built around a court with a fountain. And the whole was embellished with columns, statues, marbles.

Art and taste pervaded this delightful haven but the dominating feature was water which refreshed and reflected the momentary pleasures in seemingly endless repetition. There were also an Imperial Palace, Libraries, The Terrace of Tempe. Now only the ruins together with a few endeavours at reconstruction remain. A vague sense of irony strikes the visitor at the thought of Hadrian, the emperor-god, whose sole end in projecting and building it had been that of eternal pleasure.

Returning, we ascend the slope toward Tivoli.

The asphalted road winds beneath olive trees growing among rocks. Below is the Roman countryside slightly undulating toward Rome and the sea.

We are now in Tivoli.

Villa d'Este (Card. Ippolito d'Este. P. Ligorio, 1550)

If the 500 fountains, with their highly varied and original forms represent the most striking element of the renowned Italian villa, its position constitutes an equally important factor. The luxuriant vegetation of the villa, oriented northwards, makes it a veritable oasis and thousands of water spouts fill the sheltered valley with sweet freshness providing a spectacular sight. The inspiring beauty of Villa d'Este springs from its contrast with its scorched surroundings. Here too, art and taste have bent nature to the creation of beauty; the Estense family had for a long time been builders of pleasure retreats (Ferrara. Palazzo Schifanoia = Carefree) made to drive away the boredom of interminable days.

Yet a strikling contrast seems to divide Hadrian's concept from Card. Ippolito's. Hadrian's villa is luxurious and worldly, Card. Ippolito's, with its beautiful fountains, achieves an almost spiritual character.

Temple of Vesta (or of the Sibyl)

It is a building of great beauty noteworthy for the choice columns and artistically precious capitals, and is particularly impressive owing to its position: rising high above the cliff, it dominates the small valley.

The Temple goes back to the last period of the Republic and the name of the divinity to whom it was dedicated is not known with any degree of certainty.

Within the gates of **Villa Gregoriana** are the famous cascades of the Aniene river.

Of varying importance historically, archaeologically and artistically, the following places provide highlights of interest to the visitor.

On the via Aurelia: Cervèteri and, to the right, Bracciano.

In the Castelli Romani zone: Palestrina (once Praeneste), as ancient as the ruins of its Temple of Fortuna Primigenia, and important throughout Mediaeval and Renaissance history.

Frascati with its renowned Renaissance villas: Aldobrandini, Falconieri, Torlonia.

Grottaferrata, famous for its abbey; Castel Gandolfo and Marino.

HELPFUL HINTS

Arrival in Rome

The city of Rome fulfills two distinct purposes: capital of the Italian Republic for one, and, on a universal plane, seat of the papacy and capital of Christianity. A centre of attraction for the population of the centre-south of the peninsula and for all peoples of the Christian world, it reveals the ferment of a city whose population has surpassed the two million mark though ordered and contained within the limits of Christian tradition; and it manifests through its variegated international clergy its mission of instruction and civilization. The sacred aspect which dominates the city, evident in its festivals, in the encounters with the Pope in Piazza S. Pietro, in the district processions, is often in direct contrast with the worldly tone of some streets — v. Veneto, Piazza di Spagna, Piazza del Popolo —, where a dazzling elegant crowd, of film and international origin, meets to converse, read, gossip. The present day character of Rome lies in these contrasts. In any case it is ever a city rooted in the past. To really get to know it, one should stroll the streets of Campo Marzio, dine in an osteria in Trastevere, pause around noontime in Piazza Colonna, walk up Via Veneto, happen upon a procession in the S. Giovanni quarter, promenade along the Appian Way at sunset. It is a city of many faces, now mysterious like many of the pages of her history, now open like the gestures of her people. She is always attractive and fleeting, simple and enigmatic. Rome, in its human, urban fibre, is a summing up of the civilizations of the world.

PRACTICAL NOTES

Arrival by rail. From the train we note the profound contrast between the modern city — train tracks, blocks of flats — and its past, with its ruins and ancient buildings.

AT THE STATION

If you are booked with a Tourist Agency. A uniformed representative wearing the badge of the company will be there to meet you. Should he be delayed have your baggage removed from the train and await him in the station from where he will accompany you to your hotel.

Travellers with hotel reservations. A simple telephone call before leaving for Rome will insure the presence of a hotel representative on arrival. He will meet you at the entrance to the station where he will then take charge of everything.

Travellers with no hotel reservations. Call a porter — they are identifiable by the number on their jacket — who will carry your baggage to the station entrance. Distinguishable by the name they bear on their cap or sleeve are the many hotel representatives who are there to greet arriving travellers and to accompany them or to indicate the most convenient route to the hotel or pension.

If you are travelling alone and wish to reach a hotel or district of the city by taxi. Walk off the platform, through the station, and outside in the square taxis are waiting. Should you have a great deal of luggage a porter will accompany you. Make certain to take his number in case of loss.

If you are travelling alone and wish to reach a hotel or district of the city by means of public transport. Just outside, in the square before the station, walk to the tram or bus stop.

Arrival by car

All parts of Rome may be reached from the motorway that surrounds the city at a distance of about 20 Km. Once on this motorway follow the signs indicating the many entrance-exits.

Bear in mind the following traffic directions:

To and from the North: Flaminia, Salaria;

To and from the South and the sea: Appia Nuova, via Cristoforo Colombo, Ostiense;

To and from the East: Nomentana, Tiburtina;

To and from Trastevere and the Tyrrhenian coast: Aurelia.

Within the walls, follow the signs indicating the various areas of the city. To exit from the city, first proceed in any direction until you come upon a green road sign indicating **Firenze-Napoli,** the opposite — North, South — directions of the Autostrada del Sole. Along the motorway other signs indicate further directions.

Along the motorway and in town remember that there is a speed limit. On arrival in town, stop at tourist office or news-stand and request a **parking disk** (Disco Orario) given free. Remember that Rome is not adapted to sustain heavy modern traffic, thus in many areas the situation is difficult and at times dangerous. Attention to: speed limits, one way streets, parking areas with definite time limits (your parking disk should be visibly exposed inside the car near the windscreen and should indicate the time of arrival). Baggage should not be left in the car in an unattended zone.

In case of an accident call the Highway Patrol (page 132) and, for repairs, the Highway Assistance.

Arrival by air

From the airport you will be taken to the Terminal from where hotels or other places are easily reached.

AT THE HOTEL

The staff are prepared to serve you and speak your language.

Tips vary according to the type of hotel or restaurant. Bear in mind that both overtipping and undertipping are equal blunders. The following may serve to indicate an average which may vary according to place and circumstance.

Lift boy - L. 200
Concièrge - L. 2.000
Waiter - 10%

Also remember that tipping is customary, although not obligatory: there is always a service charge included in the bill.

Concièrge. The gold crossed keys worn on the lapel are the badge of the concièrge who often enjoys a high reputation in his setting. Some are distinguished by their personal talents and are very well known. In any case it is they who deal directly with the guests and often they have a way of opening even the most difficult doors, and not necessarily in their own interests; and they skilfully direct tourist traffic, from one part of Italy to another and throughout Europe.

PUBLIC TRANSPORTATION

Consult the A.T.A.C. Map.

Centre, 39; 64. **Trionfale,** 45, 45 b, 47 b, 99. **Prati,** 28 b, 77. **Primavalle,** 46, 47, 50, 147, 247, 247 b. **Aurelio,** 34, 42, 49, 146, 246, 346, 446, 546. **Gianicolense,** 26, 27, 41, 43, 44, 98, 98 c, 144. **Monteverde,** 75, 96, 96 c, 97 c, 128, 228, 328. **Ostiense,** 22, 23, 92, 95, 123, 223, 318. **E.U.R.,** 93, 93 b, 93 c, 94, 97, 193, 196, 197, 293, 393, 493, 593, 693. **Ardeatino,** 36 b, 91. **Appio Latino,** 18, 87, 88, 89, 90, 118, 218. **Tuscolano,** 16, 85. **Prenestino,** 81, 112, 312, 312 b, 412, 512, 612. **Centocelle,** 113, 114. **Tiburtino,** 15, 71, 109, 111, 163, 309, 311, 411. **Nomentano,** 6, 8, 8 b, 9, 35, 56, 57, 61, 135, 235, 62, 63, 65, 66, 67, 67 b, 209, 211, 409, 509. **Pietralata,** 212, 214. **Monte Sacro,** 36, 37, 38, 38 b, 58, 60, 136, 137, 237, 335, 337, 437, 537. **Pinciano,** 30. **Parioli,** 3, 4, 52, 53, 55. **Flaminio,** 20, 21. **Tor di Quinto,** 1. **Tomba di Nerone,** 2, 2 b. **Della Vittoria,** 28, 31, 32, 48, 70, 78, 201, 301.

STEFER. A1 **Ardeatino.** A2 **Capannelle.** A3 **Ciampino.** C1 **Mirti.** C2 **Torre Angela.** C3 **Villaggio Breda.** C4 **Borgata Finocchio.** C5 **Torre Spaccata.** C6 **Tor della Monaca.** T1 **Via dei Lentuli.** T2 **Viale T. Labieno.** T3 **P.C. Lavoro.** T3r **Torre Spaccata.** T4 **Cinecittà.**

SUBWAYS. For Routes and Timetables, request informations at any subway station.

Taxis are stationed in many parts of the city or you may want to telephone.

First contact with the city

To the alert visitor, suddenly in contact with Rome direct from his native land, those elements which characterize her make an immediate impact: her climate and light, bells and walls, cafés and parks. He is, though, prepared for the summons of the ancient city, the fascination of the heroic age of Christianity, the manifest greatness of the papacy and its obscure withdrawal in the following centuries. Owing to the short time allowed most visitors it would be well to penetrate the city's life, lend an ear to the heated conversations of its inhabitants, observe the gestures and flashing eyes, the ever-present warm human contact. In fact, the city you are now admiring is the natural creation of that type of man.

Climate and light. Light is one of the typical elements of the Italian landscape, and it varies from city to city, becoming clearer and more brilliant the farther south you go. It, together with the climate, has a profound influence on the people and their works, especially from an artistic point of view: they are reflected in painting and urban development, in sculpture and music. Rome is a city of the south and enjoys a «Mediterranean» climate, mild and temperate in the four seasons with periodic rainfalls of brief duration. Snow is nearly unknown. The open, high skies are, especially on summer nights, of a spectacular Mediterranean blue.

Bells. Just as the modern industrial city has its sirens which signal, in the various establishments, the start and close of the workday, so in the ancient one where religious interest predominated the varied and repeated sounds of the bells ordered the life of the inhabitants. At Rome, nowadays, the howling of sirens and the sound of bells are mixed, but the latter still prevails emphasizing once again the fascination of the past.

Walls. These structures surround the city, now in regular ordered pattern, now interrupted by buildings, or the black stumps of lava blocks lying askew, isolated in the midst of flower beds even amid ultra-modern constructions. The Aurelian was the first, the Servian Wall the second: and between the two dates of their construction lie the period of expansion through conquest, the greatness and the decline of ancient Rome.

Cafés. Roman cafés open onto the street and overflow the pavements with their tables and clients. They are the best places to sit and penetrate a particular social class and its virtues and defects. They are a characteristic of the city and it is advisable to stop there long enough to sip an espresso.

Parks. The city is full of green spaces, particularly among the ruins and were planted during the last centuries. The ilex and the maritime pine are essential elements of the Roman landscape, and fill the air with their penetrating perfume.

MEALS, FOOD, WINES

It is well to bear in mind that in Italy two principal meals are consumed, one around noontime known as pranzo, or dinner — 12:30—14:30 — and the other in the evening called cena, or supper — 20:30—22:30. Breakfasts are usually limited to coffee. Italians are partial to snacks, a glass of wine, aperitif or liqueur.

In Italy, spaghetti is but a preparatory dish to the principal meat or fish course, followed by cheese and fruit. During the meal wine is usually drunk — beer or water rarely — and caffè-espresso, believed to be a digestive, is taken at the end.

Zucchero — sugar	Vino — wine
Carne — meat	Acqua — water
Vitello — veal	Birra — beer
Limone — lemon	Pane — bread
Agnello — lamb	Tè — tea
Salsa di pomodoro — tomato sauce	Latte — milk
Formaggio — cheese	Burro — butter
Caffè — black coffee	Manzo — beef
Marmellata — marmalade or jam	Insalata — salad
Frutta — fruit	Piatto — dish
Bicchiere — water glass	Forchetta — fork
Cucchiaio — spoon	Ragù — meat sauce
Coltello — knife	

Restaurants Trattorias; Rotisseries Pizzerias

Restaurants and trattorias are places where full meals are served and the prices, apart from the cost of the meal itself, are keyed to the level of service. De luxe restaurants serve meals from L. 12.500 per person, plus service charge and taxes; the trattorias usually start at L. 7.000 per person plus service charge and taxes. These prices, of course, are merely examples, and it is possible to eat much more cheaply. Whether you stand or sit, pizzerias and rotisseries permit you to sample inexpensively the specialities of the Roman cuisine without feeling obliged to consume an entire meal.

Specialities of the Roman cuisine

The Italian cuisine is extremely varied, rather spicy, well garnished and therefore tasty and appetizing. Warning to the uninitiated: certain dishes may present difficulties to digestion. The many specialities include: cannelloni = large stuffed macaroni, rigatoni alla pagliata; spaghetti alla carbonara with bacon strips and raw egg yolk; spaghetti all'amatriciana, tomatoes and ginger; alla carrettiera.

Before ordering ask what each dish comprises. Main courses: abbacchio al forno = roast spring lamb; porchetta — roast pork; saltimbocca alla romana = slices of veal wrapped in fine strips of prosciutto and sage leaves. The many varieties of salad are excellent.

The wines generally drunk in Rome are from the Castelli, in the hill towns, and are red or white, dry or sweet.

Rome by day

Even for the visitor whose stay exceeds that of the average tourist, I still believe the chief interests are those of knowing the monuments and the people. The people can best be observed in three places: in church, at the marketplace and during the passeggiata or promenade.

In **church,** the Roman, like all Italians, displays notable individuality. The faithful, in fact, do not perform collectively, but highlight the successive ritual phases with personal gestures and so it is not uncommon to see some kneeling, others standing, still others with head bowed or gazing on high. Roundabout the devout, one notes much stir and noise.

The **Market** is dominated by shouts, deafening hubbub and the bawling of the vendors, who give the passerby little time to reflect. The markets of Piazza Vittorio, Campo dei Fiori, Porta Portese, each with its own characteristic products, environment and clientele, are perhaps the most typical expression of the talkative and pungent, jovial and jesting Roman.

But his public demeanour may be seen above all in the **passeggiata.** In via Ripetta, dei Condotti, del Babuino, from 11 to 12; at twilight along the Corso or at night in via Tritone, Piazza Barberini and via Veneto, the Roman is ever ready with a witticism, a dry remark or a jovial comment among friends when a pretty girl or an eccentric type goes by . . . Furnished with inexhaustible invention he flings them to all and sundry and awaits the results.

The Roman spirit is the fruit of a secular tradition. The promenade may also take place in panoramic areas — Pincio, Monte Mario, Janiculum — and in the numerous parks of the city, such as those of Villas Borghese and Sciarra.

Sports and entertainment

Following is a list of places where the visitors may spend an afternoon or evening enjoying a sporting event. Don't miss the pleasure of attending a soccer game (calcio), not so much for the sport itself as for the lively, colourful spectacle offered by the crowd. Boxing matches take place in the Palazzetto dello Sport and, at the EUR, the Olimpic Sports Palace; race tracks: Tor di Quinto, delle Capannelle and Tor di Valle.

Rome by night

Rome, as centre of Christianity, maintains the tone of a holy city and so even entertainments and artistic manifestations are kept within limits. The city, however, does offer everything from the world's most vital type of film, there are 200 movie theatres — Rome is the Italian film capital: Cinecittà — to the typical atmosphere created in a trattoria by two strolling musicians. Between these two limits lies that captivating spectacle called « sound and light » which, during the season, takes place in the Roman Forum, in Hadrian's Villa at Tivoli and in Villa Torlonia at Frascati. The spectacle is an attempt to evoke historical figures and in some cases the effects are truly successful.

Moreover, there are the theatres, cafés and orchestras.

TIMETABLE: CHURCHES - CATACOMBS - MUSEUMS

The visitor is advised to call before going.

Churches	Minor: during the services Principal: until noon and from 16.00 on. Tip the sacristan for illumination.
Ara Pacis Augusti (Via Ripetta)	W. 10-16. S. 9-13; 15-18 Sundays 9-13. Closed: Mondays
Baths of Caracalla (V. Terme Carac.)	9-Sunset
Castel Sant'Angelo (Lung. Castello, 1 - Tel. 6 50 36)	9-13. Closed: Mondays

CATACOMBS

Domitilla (V. d. 7 Chiese, 282. Tel. 5 11 03 42)	W. 8-12; 14,30-17,30. S. 8-12; 14,30-18 Closed: Tuesdays
Priscilla (V. Salaria, 430. Tel. 8 38 04 08)	W. 8-12; 14,30-17,30. S. 9-12; 14,30-18
St. Callixtus (V. Appia Antica, 110. Tel. 5 13 67 25)	W. 8,30-12; 14,30-17. S. 9-12; 15-19 Closed: Wednesdays
St. Sebastian (V. Appia Antica, 132. Tel. 73 98 34)	W. 8,30-12; 14,30-17. S. 9-12; 15-19
Pretestato (V. Appia Antica)	9-12; 14,30-Sunset
S. Agnese (V. Nomentana, 285. Tel. 8 31 91 40)	9-12; 15,30-17
Colosseum (Piazza del Colosseo)	9-17
Domus Aurea (V. Labicana)	9-13. Closed: Mondays
Farnesina, National Cabinet of Engravings (V. Lungara, 230. Tel. 5 46 05 65)	9-13

FORUMS

Caesar's (V. d. Fori Imperiali)	10-17. Sundays 9-13 Closed: Mondays
Roman-Palatine (V. d. Fori Imperiali. Tel. 6 79 03 33)	W. 9-16. S. 9-17 Closed: Tuesdays
Trajan's, Trajan's Markets (V. IV Novembre) **Augustus', Nerva's,** **House of the Knights of Rhodes** (V. d. Campo Carleo)	W. 10-17. S. 9-13; 15-18 Sundays 9-13 Closed: Mondays

GALLERIES

Colonna (V. d. Pilotta, 14. Tel. 6 79 43 62)	Saturdays 9-17
Doria-Pamphili (P. d. Collegio Romano, 1-A. Tel. 6 79 43 65)	10-13 Closed: Mondays, Wednesdays, Thursdays

Farnese (P. Farnese, 67. Tel. 56 52 41)	Sundays 11-12
National (Pal. Barberini) (V. 4 Fontane, 13. Tel. 4 75 45 91)	9-14. Sundays 9-13 Closed: Mondays
National of Ancient Art (V. d. Lungara, 10. Tel. 6 54 23 23)	9-14. Sundays 9-13
National of Modern Art (V.le d. Belle Arti, 131. Tel. 80 27 51)	8,30-13,30. Sundays 9,30-13,30 Closed: Mondays
Spada (P. Capo di Ferro, 3. Tel. 6 56 11 58)	9-13,30. Sundays 9-13 Closed: Mondays
Goethe Museum and Gallery (V. d. Corso, 17. Tel. 6 79 40 94)	10-13; 16-19. Sundays 10-13 Closed: Mondays
Hadrian's Villa (Tivoli)	9-17 Closed: Mondays
Keats' House (P. di Spagna, 26. Tel. 6 78 42 35)	W. 9-12,30; 14,30-16. S. 9-12; 16-18 Closed: Saturdays, Sundays and Holidays

MUSEUMS

Barracco (C.so Vittorio Emanuele, 158. Tel. 6 54 08 45)	9-14. Sundays 9-13. Closed: Mondays. Tuesdays, Thursdays 9-14; 17-20
Borghese and Gallery (P.le Museo Borghese, 3. Tel. 85 85 77)	9-14. Sundays 9-13. Closed: Mondays
Centrale Risorgimento (V. S. Pietro in Carcere. Tel. 6 79 35 26)	Wednesdays, Fridays, Sundays 10-13
Israelite (Lung Cenci. Tel. 6 56 46 48)	10-14. Closed: Saturdays
Roman Civilization (P. G. Agnelli, E.U.R. Tel. 59 60 41)	9-14. Sundays 9-13 Tuesdays, Thursdays 9-13; 15-18
Palazzo Venezia (P. Venezia, 3. Tel. 6 79 88 65)	9-14. Sundays 9-13 Closed: Mondays
di Roma (P. S. Pantaleo. Tel. 65 58 80)	9-14. Sundays 9-13
Vatican and Galleries (Tel. 6 98 33 33)	W. 9-14. (1/7-30/9): 9-17. Closed: Sundays and Holidays
Nazionale Romano or delle Terme (V. d. Terme d. Diocleziano. Tel. 48 93 19)	8,30-14. Sundays 9-13 Closed: Mondays
National of Villa Giulia (P. Villa Giulia, 9. Tel. 3 60 19 51)	9-14. Sundays 9-13 Closed: Mondays
Capitoline and Picture Gallery (P. d. Campidoglio, 1. Tel. 67 10)	9-14. Tuesdays, Thursdays 9-14; 17-20 Saturdays 9-14; 20,30-23
Ostia Antica	10-17
Palestrina (T. Fortuna Primigenia)	9,30-15,30. Sundays 9-13 Closed: Mondays
Quirinal (Palace)	14-17
Tabularium (V. d. Campidoglio)	10-13. Closed: Mondays
Villa d'Este (Tivoli) (Tel. 0774/2 20 70)	9-Two hours before sunset Closed: Mondays. Evening Visit with Foun- tain Illumination
Villa Medici (V.le Trinità d. Monti, 1)	Visit of the Garden: Wednesdays unless a holiday: 9-11

EMBASSIES

Afghanistan - V. C. Fea, 1 - Tel. 85 68 98
Albania - V. Asmara, 9 - Tel. 8 38 07 25
Algeria - V. d. Villa Ricotti, 20 - Tel. 42 93 51 - 42 93 52
Argentina - P. Esquilino, 2 - Tel. 48 25 51
Australia - V. Alessandria, 215 - Tel. 84 12 41
Austria - V. G. B. Pergolesi, 3 - Tel. 86 82 41
Bangladesh - V. A. Bertoloni, 14 - Tel. 80 35 95 - 87 85 41
Belgium - V. Mt. Parioli, 49 - Tel. 3 60 94 41 - 2 - 3 - 4 - 5
Bolivia - V. Archimede, 143 - Tel. 80 42 28
Brazil - P. Navona, 14 - Tel. 65 08 41
Bulgaria - V. Rubens, 21 - Tel. 85 64 38
Burma - V. Bellini, 20 - Tel. 85 93 74
Canada - V. G. B. De Rossi, 27 - Tel. 85 53 42
Central African Rep. - V. G. Pisanelli, 4 - Tel. 3 60 04 88
Ceylon - V. G. Cuboni, 6 - Tel. 87 45 02 - 80 53 62
Chile - V. Panisperna, 207 - Tel. 46 04 92
Chinese People's Rep. - V. Bruxelles, 56 - Tel. 86 72 94
Colombia - V. G. Pisanelli, 4 - Tel. 3 60 27 04 - 3 60 19 59
Costarica - Lung. Flaminio, 24 - Tel. 3 60 06 74
Cuba - V. Licinia, 7 - Tel. 57 21 68
Cyprus - V. Meropia, 78 - Tel. 5 13 41 44
Czechoslovakia - V. d. Colli d. Farnesina, 144 - Tel. 3 27 87 41
Denmark - V. Monte Parioli, 6 - Tel. 3 60 04 41 - 3 60 04 42
Dominican Rep. - V. Romagna, 26 - Tel. 4 75 90 30
Ecuador - V. G. d'Arezzo, 14 - Tel. 85 17 84 - 85 22 29
Egypt - V. Salaria, 267 - Tel. 85 61 93 - 85 74 20
Ethiopia - V. Tartaglia, 11 - Tel. 87 53 88
Finland - V.le G. Rossini, 18 - Tel. 85 83 29
France - V. Giulia, 251 - Tel. 6 56 52 41
Gabon - L. A. Vessella, 31 - Tel. 83 64 61 - 83 15 91
German Democratic Rep. - V. Frasone, 55 - Tel. 46 58 78
German Federal Rep. - V. Po, 25c - Tel. 86 03 41 - 86 93 41 - 85 68 06
Ghana Rep. - V. Ostriana, 4 - Tel. 83 60 74
Great Britain - V. XX Settembre, 80a - Tel. 4 75 54 41
Greece - V.le G. Rossini, 4 - Tel. 85 96 30
Guatemala - V. Archimede, 35 - Tel. 80 39 36
Guinea - V. L. Luciani, 41 - Tel. 3 60 88 95
Haiti - V. R. Fauro, 59 - Tel. 87 27 77
Holy See - V. Po, 27 - Tel. 86 72 87
Hungary - V. d. Villini, 12-16 - Tel. 86 30 68 - 85 87 72
India - V. V. XX Settembre, 5 - Tel. 46 46 42
Indonesia - V. Campania, 55 - Tel. 4 75 92 51 - 46 55 10
Iran - V. Nomentana, 361 - Tel. 8 39 02 41
Iraq - V. Pisanelli, 25 - Tel. 3 60 89 57
Ireland - V. d. Pozzetto, 105 - Tel. 6 78 25 41 - 2
Israel - V. M. Mercati, 12-14 - Tel. 87 45 41 - 2
Ivory Coast Rep. - V. L. Spallanzani, 4-6 - Tel. 86 80 40
Japan - V. Q. Sella, 58 - Tel. 4 75 73 23 - 4 75 74 53

Jordan - V. G. d'Arezzo, 5 - Tel. 85 73 96 - 86 24 97

Korea - V. B. Oriani, 30 - Tel. 80 53 06

Kuwait - P. Montegrappa, 4 - Tel. 3 60 38 41 - 2

Lebanon - V. L. Settembrini, 38 - Tel. 3 59 58 48 - 49

Liberia - V.le B. Buozzi, 61 - Tel. 80 58 10 - 80 58 12

Libya - V. Nomentana, 365 - Tel. 83 09 51 - 2 - 3 - 4 - 5; 8 31 01 57

Luxemburg - V. Guerrieri, 3 - Tel. 5 74 54 56

Malaysia - V. L. Spallanzani, 8 - Tel. 85 57 64 - 85 36 28

Malta - Lung. Marzio, 12 - Tel. 65 94 97 - 65 99 90 - 65 76 29

Mexico - V. L. Spallanzani, 16 - Tel. 85 40 93 - 85 76 08

Monaco - V. A. Bertoloni, 36 - Tel. 80 33 61

Morocco - V. d. Scialoja, 32 - Tel. 3 61 12 23 - 3 61 12 21

New Zealand - V. Zara, 28 - Tel. 8 44 86 73 - 8 44 86 96

Netherlands - V. M. Mercati, 8 - Tel. 87 31 41 - 2 - 3 - 4 - 5

Nicaragua - V. Pizio, 11 - Tel. 32 07 75

Nigeria - P. Novella, 1 - Tel. 8 38 02 90

Norway - V. d. Terme Deciane, 10 - Tel. 57 87 46 - 57 22 97

Pakistan - Lung. d. Armi, 22 - Tel. 31 14 70 - 31 10 07

Panama - V. Po, 10 - Tel. 8 44 55 89

Paraguay - V. E. De' Cavalieri, 12 - Tel. 8 44 82 36

Peru - V. Po, 22 - Tel. 85 65 56

Philippines - V. S. Valentino, 12 - Tel. 80 35 30 - 80 35 31

Poland - V. P. P. Rubens, 20 - Tel. 3 60 94 55 - 3 60 95 97

Portugal - V. G. Pezzana, 9 - Tel. 87 94 86 - 87 38 01

Rumania - V. N. Tartaglia, 36 - Tel. 80 45 29 - 80 44 23

Salvador - P.le d. Belle Arti, 1 - Tel. 3 60 18 53

San Marino - V. Duse, 35 - Tel. 80 45 67

Saudi Arabia - V.le Regina Margherita, 260 - Tel. 86 81 61

Senegal - V. Tagliamento, 45 - Tel. 85 94 97

Sierra Leone - V. Asmara, 5 - Tel. 8 31 50 51 - 8 31 50 53

Somaliland - V. d. Gracchi, 303 - Tel. 35 00 52 - 3 59 98 64

South Africa - P. Montegrappa, 4 - Tel. 3 60 84 41 - 3 60 58 63

Sovereign Order of Malta - Lung. Marzio, 12 - Tel. 65 94 97

Spain - Largo Fontanella Borghese, 19 - Tel. 6 79 85 07 - 6 79 85 06

Sudan - V. d. Porta Ardeatina, 1 - Tel. 7 57 33 44

Sweden - P. Rio de Janeiro, 3 - Tel. 86 04 41 - 2 - 3

Switzerland - V. B. Oriani, 61 - Tel. 80 36 41 - 2 - 3 - 4 - 5

Tanzanian Rep. - V. G. B. Vico, 9 - Tel. 3 61 08 98

Thailand - V. Nomentana, 132 - Tel. 83 70 73 - 8 31 96 90 - 5 03 08 04

Tunisia - V. Asmara, 7 - Tel. 8 99 07 48

Turkey - V. Palestro, 28 - Tel. 48 14 35

United States - V. V. Veneto, 119 - Tel. 46 74

Uruguay - V. V. Veneto, 183 - Tel. 49 27 96

U.S.S.R. - V. Gaeta, 5 - Tel. 48 13 89

Venezuela - V.le B. Buozzi, 109 - Tel. 87 25 52 - 87 74 03

Viet-Nam - P. Barberini, 12 - Tel. 4 75 52 86 - 4 75 40 98

Yemen - V. Taro, 37 - Tel. 85 50 88

Yugoslavia - V. Mt. Parioli, 20 - Tel. 3 60 08 05 - 3 60 07 96

Zaire - V. Mecenate, 24 - Tel. 7 31 23 08

Zambia - V. E. Q. Visconti, 8 - Tel. 31 22 97 - 31 03 40

OPENING HOURS

Chemists: Hours: Nights or holidays - See newspaper listings.
Banks: 8.30-13.30 - Closed: Saturdays and holidays.
Ladies' hairdressers: Closed: Sundays.
Barbers: Closed: Sundays and Mondays.
Telephones: Central Office: Sta. Maria in Via from 8-22.
Electrical Current: 125 V. and 220 V.
Shops: 9-13; 16-19.30.

EMERGENCY TELEPHONE NUMBERS

Car Removal - Tel. 6 78 07 41/2/3
Emergency Assistance - Tel. 1 13
Firemen - Tel. 4 44 41 - 4 44 44
First Aid (Red Cross) - Tel. 51 00
Highway Assistance - Tel. 1 16
Highway Patrol - Tel. 55 66 66
Lost and Found - Tel. 5 81 60 40
Night Medical Emergency Service - Tel. 48 01 58 - 4 75 00 10
Railway Enquiries - Tel. 47 75
Taxi - Tel. 84 33

GENERAL PAPAL AUDIENCES

Take place an Wednesdays at 12. Permits may be obtained from Monsignor Maestro di Camera di Sua Santità, whose office is located within the Bronze Door (from 9-2:30). The visitor should have a letter of introduction from his parish priest.

CATHOLIC CHURCHES: MASSES

Tourist Masses: Church of Sacro Cuore, Via Marsala: Every half hour from 5:30.

S. Agata (Ireland) - Via S. Agata dei Goti - **S. Andrea** (Scotland) - Via Quattro Fontane - **S. Antonio** (Portugal) - Via S. Antonio dei Portoghesi - **S. Antonio** (Russia) - V. C. Alberto - **S. Carlino** (Spain) - Via Quirinale - **S. Giorgio** (England) - Via S. Sebastiano - **S. Girolamo** (Yugoslavia) - Via di Ripetta - **S. Giuliano** (Belgium) - Via del Sudario - **S. Luigi** (France) - Piazza S. Luigi dei Francesi - **S. Maria dell'Anima** (Austria) - Via dell'Anima - **S. Maria della Pietà** (Germany) - Via della Sagrestia - **SS. Addolorata** (Argentina) - Piazza Buenos Aires - **S. Stanislao** (Poland) - Via Delle Botteghe Oscure - **S. Stefano** (Hungary) - Via S. Stefano - **S. Susanna** (USA) - Piazza S. Bernardo.

NON-CATHOLIC CHURCHES

Adventist - Lungotevere Michelangelo, 7
American - Via Nazionale
Anglican - Via del Babuino, 153
Baptist - Piazza S. Lorenzo in Lucina, 35
Evangelican «Assembly of God» - Via dei Bruzi, 11
Evangelican Italian Methodist - Via Firenze, 38
Evangelican Lutheran - Via Toscana, 7
Presbyterian - Via XX Settembre, 7
Russian Orthodox - Via Palestro, 71
Synagogue - Lungotevere dei Cenci
Waldensian - Via IV Novembre, 107

HOTELS

Hotels de Luxe

		Tel.
Ambasciatori Palace	Via Vittorio Veneto, 70	47 38 31
Bernini - Bristol	Piazza Barberini, 23	46 30 51
Cavalieri Hilton	Via Cadlolo, 101	31 51
Eden	Via Ludovisi, 49	48 05 51
Excelsior	Via Vittorio Veneto, 125	47 08
Hassler - Villa Medici	Piazza Trinità de' Monti, 6	6 79 26 51
Le Grand Hotel et de Rome	Via Vitt. Emanuele Orlando, 3	47 09

First class

Anglo - Americano	Via 4 Fontane, 12	47 29 41
Atlantico	Via Cavour, 23	48 59 51
Beverly - Hills	Largo Benedetto Marcello, 220	85 21 41
Borromini	Via Lisbona, 7	84 13 21
Boston	Via Lombardia, 47	4 75 15 92
Cardinal	Via Giulia, 62	6 54 42 89
Cicerone	Via Cicerone, 55	35 76
Claridge	Viale Liegi, 62	86 85 56
Commodore	Via Torino, 1	4 75 15 15
De la Ville	Via Sistina, 69	6 79 89 41
Delle Nazioni	Via Poli, 7	6 79 24 41
Delta	Via Labicana, 144	77 00 21
D'Inghilterra	Via Bocca di leone, 14	6 78 11 51
Eliseo	Via di Porta Pinciana, 30	46 05 56
Flora	Via Vittorio Veneto, 191	49 78 21
Forum	Via Tor de' Conti, 25	6 79 24 46
Giulio Cesare	Via degli Scipioni, 287	31 02 44
Hermitage	Via E. Vajna, 12	87 00 73
Holiday Inn	Via Aurelia Antica, 415	58 72
Holiday Inn Eur	Via della Magliana, 821	54 75
Imperiale	Via Vittorio Veneto, 24	4 75 63 51
Jolly	Corso d'Italia, 1	84 95
Leonardo da Vinci	Via dei Gracchi, 324	38 20 91
Londra e Cargill	Piazza Sallustio, 18	47 38 71
Lord Byron	Via G. De Notaris, 5	3 60 95 41
Majestic	Via Vittorio Veneto, 50	48 68 41
Marc'Aurelio	Via Gregorio XI, 135	6 23 05 24
Marini Strand	Via del Tritone, 17	6 79 39 41
Massimo D'Azeglio	Via Cavour, 18	46 06 46
Mediterraneo	Via Cavour, 15	46 40 51
Metropole	Via Principe Amedeo, 3	4 75 14 41
Michelangelo	Via Stazione di S. Pietro, 14	63 12 51
Midas Palace	Via Aurelia, 800	65 06
Milano	Piazza Montecitorio, 12	6 78 90 11
Mondial	Via Torino, 127	47 28 61
Napoleon	Piazza Vitt. Emanuele, 105	73 76 46
Nazionale	Piazza Montecitorio, 131	6 78 92 51
Palatino	Via Cavour, 213	4 75 47 11
Parco dei Principi	Via G. Frescobaldi, 5	84 10 71
Plaza	Via del Corso, 126	6 79 77 51
President	Via Emanuele Filiberto, 173	77 01 21
Quirinale	Via Nazionale, 7	48 91 01
Raphael	Largo Febo, 2	6 56 90 51
Regina Carlton	Via Vittorio Veneto, 72	4 75 88 41
Residence Palace	Via Archimede, 69	87 83 41
Ritz	Piazza Euclide, 43	80 37 51
Royal Santina	Via Marsala, 22	4 95 52 41
San Giorgio	Via G. Amendola, 61	4 75 13 41
Savoia	Via Ludovisi, 15	48 71 41
Shangri La' Corsetti	Viale Algeria, 141	5 91 64 41
The Regency	Via Romagna, 42	4 75 92 81
Universo	Via Principe Amedeo, 5-b	4 75 05 42
Valadier	Via della Fontanella, 15	6 79 69 66
Victoria	Via Campania, 41	48 00 52
Villa Pamphili	Via della Nocetta, 105	58 62
Ville Radieuse	Via Aurelia, 641	6 23 03 41
Visconti Palace	Via Federico Cesi, 37	36 84

Accademia	Piazza Accademia San Luca, 75	6 79 22 66
Adriano	Via di Pallacorda, 2	6 54 24 51
Alexandra	Via Vittorio Veneto, 18	46 19 43
Alpi	Via Castelfidardo, 84-a	46 46 18
American Palace Eur	Via Laurentina, 554	5 91 15 51
Arcangelo	Via Boezio, 15	31 10 98
Archimede	Via dei Mille, 19	4 95 46 00
Astor	Via Tevere, 5-d	85 12 24
Atlante	Via Vitelleschi, 34	6 56 41 96
Atlante Garden	Via Crescenzio, 78-a	3 59 88 84
Atlas	Via Rasella, 3	48 47 84
Autostello A.C.I.	Via C. Colombo Km. 13	6 07 09 41
Bled	Via Santa Croce in Gerusalemme, 40	77 71 02
Bolivar	Via della Cordonata, 6	6 79 16 14
Bologna	Via Santa Chiara, 4-A	6 56 89 51
Britannia	Via Napoli, 64	46 31 53
Caprice	Via Liguria, 38	46 21 88
Carriage	Via delle Carrozze, 36	6 79 51 66
Centro	Via Firenze, 12	46 41 42
Cervinia	Via Vittorio Amedeo II, 16	7 57 69 53
Cesari	Via di Pietra, 89-A	6 79 23 86
Clodio	Via Santa Lucia, 10	31 75 41
Colony - Flaminio	Via Monterosi, 18	3 27 68 43
Colosseum	Via Sforza, 10	4 75 12 28
Columbia	Via Viminale, 15	48 72 89
Columbus	Via della Conciliazione, 33	6 56 48 74
Consul	Via Aurelia, 727	6 22 26 93
Degli Aranci	Via Barnaba Oriani, 11	87 02 02
Dei Congressi	Viale Shakespeare, 29	59 60 21
Della Conciliazione	Via Borgo Pio, 164	6 56 79 10
Della Torre Argentina	Corso Vitt. Emanuele, 102	6 54 82 51
Delle Legazioni	Via Barberini, 11	4 75 16 16
Del Senato	Piazza della Rotonda, 73	6 79 32 31
Derby	Largo 7 Chiese	5 12 00 50
Diana	Via Principe Amedeo, 4	4 75 15 41
Diplomatic	Via Vittoria Colonna, 28	6 54 20 84
Dover	Via Pineta Sacchetti, 43	6 22 28 18
Esperia	Via Nazionale, 22	48 72 45
Eur Motel	Via Pontina, 416	6 48 01 95
Fenix	Viale Gorizia, 5	85 07 41
Fiamma	Via Gaeta, 61	4 75 89 12
Fiume	Via Brescia, 5	8 44 16 39
Fleming	Piazza Monteleone di Spoleto, 20	3 27 67 41
Fontana	Piazza di Trevi, 46	6 78 61 13
Galles	Viale Castro Pretorio, 66	4 95 47 41
Garden Roxy	Piazza B. Gastaldi, 4	80 30 41
Genio	Via G. Zanardelli, 28	6 54 06 60
Genova	Via Cavour, 33	46 54 51
Gerber	Via degli Scipioni, 241	3 50 51 48
Globus	Viale Ippocrate, 119	4 95 39 94
Gregoriana	Via Gregoriana, 18	6 79 42 69
Imperator	Via Aurelia, 619	6 22 22 32
Impero	Via Viminale, 19	46 44 51
Internazionale	Via Sistina, 79	6 79 30 47
King	Via Sistina, 131	46 08 78
La Capitale e Santa Maria Maggiore	Via Carlo Alberto, 3	73 38 03
La Residenza	Via Emilia, 22	6 79 95 92
Lloyd	Via Alessandria, 110-A	86 29 77
Lugano	Via Tritone, 132	46 07 33
Lux Messe	Via Volturno, 32	46 46 20
Madison	Via Marsala, 60	4 95 43 44
Madrid	Via Mario de' Fiori, 93	6 79 12 49
Medici	Via Flavia, 96	48 73 70
Milani	Via Magenta, 12	4 95 26 41
Motel Agip	S.S. n. 1 Aurelia Km. 8,400	62 68 43
Motel Americana	S.S. n. 1 Aurelia Km. 16,800	6 90 91 41
Motel Cristoforo Colombo	Via C. Colombo, 710	5 91 28 45
Nizza	Via M. D'Azeglio, 16	46 10 61
Nord-Nuova Roma	Via G. Amendola, 3	46 54 41
Nova Domus	Via G. Savonarola, 38	31 81 41
Nuova Italia	Via Como, 1	85 00 51
Olympic	Via Properzio, 2-a	31 24 60
Oxford	Via Boncompagni, 89	4 75 13 93
Pace - Elvezia	Via IV Novembre, 104	6 79 10 44

Pacific	Viale Medaglie d'Oro, 51	3 59 80 37
Panama	Via Salaria, 336	86 25 58
Parioli	Viale Bruno Buozzi, 54	87 87 41
Park	Via Alamanno Morelli, 5	87 01 84
Patria	Via Torino, 36	6 79 96 92
Piccadilly	Via Magna Grecia, 122	77 70 17
Porta Maggiore	Piazza Porta Maggiore, 25	77 91 14
Quattro Fontane	Via Quattro Fontane, 149-a	4 75 49 36
Raffaello	Via Urbana, 3	46 43 42
Raganelli	Via Aurelia, 738	6 22 30 70
Regno	Via del Corso, 331	6 79 21 62
Rest	Via Aurelia, 325	6 37 33 96
Rex	Via Torino, 149	4 75 13 10
Richmond	Largo Corrado Ricci, 36	6 78 37 97
River	Via Flaminia, 39	3 60 08 41
Rivoli	Via Taramelli, 7	87 81 40
San Giusto	Piazza Bologna, 58	42 55 83
San Marco	Via Villafranca, 1	49 04 37
San Remo	Via M. D'Azeglio, 36	46 17 41
Sant'Anna	Via Borgo Pio, 134	6 54 16 02
Santa Chiara	Via Santa Chiara, 21	6 54 17 00
Siracusa	Via Marsala, 50	4 95 78 38
Sitea	Via Vittorio Emanuele Orlando, 90	4 75 15 60
Siviglia	Via Gaeta, 12	4 75 04 24
Sole al Pantheon	Via del Pantheon, 63	6 79 33 29
Sorrento e Patrizia	Via Nazionale, 251	46 24 44
Tea	Via Sardegna, 19	6 79 93 87
Terminal	Via Principe Amedeo, 103	73 40 41
Tevere	Via Aniene, 3	85 40 78
Tirreno	Via San Martino ai Monti, 18	46 07 78
Tiziano	Corso Vittorio Emanuele, 110	65 50 87
Torino	Via Principe Amedeo, 8	4 75 47 41
Touring	Via Principe Amedeo, 34	46 53 51
Traiano	Via IV Novembre, 154	6 79 23 58
Tre Api	Via del Mancino, 12	6 78 35 00
Tritone	Via del Tritone, 210	6 78 94 44
Villa delle Rose	Via Vicenza, 5	4 95 17 88
Villa Florence	Via Nomentana, 28	85 81 38
Y.M.C.A.	Piazza Indipendenza, 23-c	46 49 21
York	Via Cavriglia, 26	8 10 22 22

Third class

A.B.C.	Via Magazzini Generali, 4	5 77 81 96
Abruzzi	Piazza della Rotonda, 69	6 79 20 21
Alba	Via Leonina, 12	48 44 71
Alicorni	Via Scossacavalli, 11	65 52 35
Aretusa	Via Gaeta, 14	4 75 56 74
Ariston	Via Filippo Turati, 16	7 31 03 41
Artis	Via Capo le Case, 10	6 79 43 15
Astoria Garden	Via Varese, 8	4 95 36 53
Aurelius	Via Aurelia, 458	6 22 80 84
Aventino	Via S. Domenico, 10	57 28 31
Bel Poggio	Via di Settebagni, 735	6 91 92 97
Bramante	Vicolo delle Palline, 24	6 54 04 26
Bridge	Viale Tirreno, 74	84 26 14
Buenos Aires	Via Clitunno, 9	86 18 39
Canada	Via Vicenza, 58	4 95 07 49
Capitol	Via G. Amendola, 77	46 26 17
Casa Kolbe	Via San Teodoro, 44	6 79 49 74
Cecil	Via Francesco Crispi, 55-a	6 79 79 96
Clipper	Via Rasella, 47	48 74 89
Concordia	Via Capo le Case, 14	6 79 56 93
Condotti	Via Mario dei Fiori, 37	6 79 46 61
Corona d'Italia	Via Napoli, 3	48 44 09
Croce di Malta	Via Borgognona, 28	6 79 54 82
Daniela	Via L. Luzzatti, 31	75 05 87
Dei Pini	Via F. Sciacci, 2-C	80 38 95
Dell'Opera	Via Principe Amedeo, 14	46 52 51
D'Este	Via Carlo Alberto, 6	73 26 23
Dinesen	Via di Porta Pinciana, 18	46 50 35
D'Italia	Via 4 Fontane, 155	4 75 16 07
Domus Maximi	Via S. Prisca, 11	57 61 35
Doria	Via Merulana, 4	73 03 56

Due Torri	Vicolo del Leonetto, 23	6 54 09 56
Edera	Via A. Poliziano, 75	73 83 84
Farnese	Via A. Farnese, 30	38 00 39
Frattina	Via Frattina, 107	6 79 20 71
Galileo	Via Palestro, 33	46 49 10
Gallia	Via di Santa Maria Maggiore, 143	4 75 47 65
Gemini	Via G. Mazzoni, 24	4 27 01 76
Giotto	Via Cardinal Passionei, 35	6 27 57 00
Grifo	Via del Boschetto, 144	48 23 23
Homs	Via délla Vite, 71	6 79 29 76
Igea	Via Principe Amedeo, 97	7 31 12 12
Ivanhoe	Via dei Ciancaleoni, 49	48 01 86
Ivanhoe (Dipendenza)	Via Urbana, 50	48 01 86
La Pergola	Via Val di Sangro, 145	8 10 69 85
La Villetta	Via Ettore Perrone, 1	75 21 59
Liberiano	Via Santa Prassede, 25	46 38 04
Locarno	Via della Penna, 22	3 61 08 41
Luciani	Via Milazzo, 8	49 06 59
Malaga	Via Udine, 12	8 44 00 67
Marconi	Via G. Amendola, 97	46 08 64
Marco Polo	Via Paolo V, 13	6 27 80 57
Margutta	Via Laurina. 34	6 79 50 57
Memphis	Via degli Avignonesi, 36-A	48 58 49
Merulana	Via Merulana, 278	48 73 13
Montagna	Via Varese, 10	4 95 33 29
Montecarlo	Via Montebello, 109	46 19 51
Monteverde e Austria	Via Monteverde, 86	53 00 00
Motel Aurora	Via Emanuele Ciaceri, 16	82 53 57
Motel Boomerang	Via Aurelia Km. 10,500	6 90 01 67
Motel Industriale	Via Tiburtina Km. 10	4 12 53 00
Mozart	Via dei Greci, 23/B	6 78 74 22
Nettuno	Via del Lavatore, 95	6 79 43 22
Nordland	Via A. Alciato, 14	6 23 18 41
Pantheon	Via dei Pastini, 131	6 79 53 05
Paradiso	Largo dei Chiavari, 79	6 56 10 03
Parker	Via Giolitti, 425	73 76 19
Parker II	Via Giolitti, 431	73 76 26
Pavia	Via Gaeta, 83	4 75 90 90
Piazza di Siena	Via S. Andrea delle Fratte, 33	6 79 61 21
Piazza di Spagna	Via Mario de' Fiori, 61	6 79 30 61
Portoghesi	Via dei Portoghesi, 1	6 56 42 31
Prati	Via Crescenzio, 87	65 53 57
Quadrifoglio	Via Giovanni Grasso, 10	6 48 02 48
Quadrifoglio II	Via Ermete Zacconi, 12	6 48 00 95
Rinascimento	Via del Pellegrino, 122	6 56 80 11
Rosen	Via Flaminia Nuova, 885	32 02 08
Salus	Piazza Indipendenza, 13	4 95 00 44
San Carlo	Via delle Carrozze, 93	6 78 45 48
San Pietro	Via Cardinale Cassetta, 9	63 08 76
San Silvestro	Via del Gambero, 3	6 79 41 69
Santa Prisca	Largo Manlio Gelsomini, 25	57 19 17
Saturnia	Via Ruinaglia, 4	46 06 28
Select	Via Varese, 6	49 11 37
Sistina	Via Sistina, 136	4 75 88 04
Smeraldo	Via dei Chiodaroli, 11	65 59 29
Souvenir	Via Terme Deciane, 3	57 09 58
Splendor	Via Luigi Luzzati, 20-a	75 54 18
Stazione	Via Gioberti, 36	7 31 12 81
Tefi	Via S. Basilio, 53	46 12 83
Touring (Dipendenza)	Via Principe Amedeo, 2	4 75 19 11
Valle	Via Cavour, 136	46 58 37
Venezia	Via Varese, 18	4 95 00 36
Verona	Via Santa Maria Maggiore, 154	46 42 90
Vienna	Via Salvatore Barzilai, 203	6 13 02 19
Villa Borghese	Via G. Sgambati, 4	86 51 84
Villa Glori	Viale del Vignola, 28	3 60 76 58
Villa Norma	Via Oglio, 8	86 48 54
Villa San Pio	Via Sant'Anselmo, 19	5 74 13 25
Viminale	Via C. Balbo, 31	48 77 28
Virgilio	Via Palermo, 30	4 75 84 51
Vulcania	Via Cavour, 117	48 58 56
Washington	Corso d'Italia, 45	8 44 16 17
Young	Via in Arcione, 77	6 79 44 69
Zara	Via IV Fontane, 37	48 74 36

		Tel.
Adua	Via dei Liguri, 7	49 01 15
Apollo	Via dei Serpenti, 109	46 58 89
Bixio	Via Bixio, 46	7 57 72 96
Cucciolo	Via Reggio Emilia, 71	85 07 97
Della Lunetta	Piazza del Paradiso, 68	6 56 10 80
Delle Regioni	Via del Tritone, 94	48 36 75
Del Popolo	Via degli Apuli, 41	49 05 58
Erice	Via Nomentana, 387	8 31 46 50
Felice	Via Tiburtina, 30	4 95 33 47
Flavio	Via Frangipane, 34	6 79 72 03
Ginevra	Via Pianciani, 17	7 57 38 09
La Flora	Via del Biscione, 6	6 54 08 65
Lodi	Via Oristano, 14	77 64 21
Molise	Via Urbana, 10-A	48 06 33
Motel La Campagnola	Via Lucio Mariani, 52	6 13 07 57
Motel Romulus	Via Salaria, 1069	8 40 17 03
Nerva	Via Tor dei Conti, 3	6 79 37 64
Palermo	Via del Gambero, 21	6 79 18 25
Perugia	Via del Colosseo, 7	6 79 72 00
Piccolo	Via dei Chiavari, 32	6 54 25 60
Pincio	Via Capo le Case, 50	6 79 12 33
Pomezia	Via dei Chiavari, 12	6 56 13 71
Provincia Romana	Largo del Pallaro, 8	6 54 10 38
Romano	Largo Corrado Ricci, 32-33	6 79 58 51
San Valentino	Via Ezio, 55	31 85 15
Sole	Via del Biscione, 76	6 54 08 73
Termini	Via G. Amendola, 77	46 43 02
Trevi	Vicolo del Babuccio, 21	6 78 95 63

PENSIONS

		First class
Caravel	Via C. Colombo, 124-c	5 11 50 46
Delle Muse	Via Tommaso Salvini, 18	87 00 95
Giolli	Via Nazionale, 69	46 23 93
La Villa	Via del Pescaccio, 101	6 23 09 80
Marcella	Via Flavia, 104	46 21 70
Terminus	Piazza della Repubblica, 47	46 15 05
Veneto	Via Piemonte, 63	48 35 20
Villa del Parco	Via Nomentana, 110	86 56 11

There are 119 second class Pensions and 236 third class Pensions

ALPHABETICAL INDEX

EDIZIONI STORTI-VENEZIA
Tel. (041) 431607

GUIDES

YELLOW SERIES	Capri Florence Naples Padua Paris Pompeii, Herculaneum and Stabiae Rome Venice Verona Jews and Synagogues
INSIDE AND OUT SERIES	Florence Pompeii Venice
MONUMENTS SERIES	The Basilica of St. Mark The Doge's Palace, Venice
MINIMA SERIES	London Pompeii The Amalfi Drive Venice
REGINA SERIES	Capri Florence, art and life Naples Pompeii, Herculaneum and Stabiae Rome Venice Verona
TREASURES SERIES	Florence Venice
GREEN SERIES	London Venice
URANIA SERIES	Painting in Venice The National Archeological Museum of Naples The Uffizi, a «Guide» to the Galleries
SIRIO SERIES	Pompeii, Eros and... Priapus

Printed in March 1983